Seven Heavens

"Profound, well-researched, and elegantly written. In this riveting narrative, Wills-Brandon shares stories of holocaust survivors, which must be told, and through these compelling stories she dispels the misconception that Judaism does not embrace the concept of an afterlife. Rather, *Seven Heavens* demonstrates how Judaism has actually chronicled near-death experiences and after-death communication for thousands of years. It is destined to become an authoritative classic in the realm of near-death-experience literature."

MARK ANTHONY, "THE PSYCHIC LAWYER" AND AUTHOR OF
THE AFTERLIFE FREQUENCY, EVIDENCE OF ETERNITY,
AND *NEVER LETTING GO*

Seven Heavens

The Afterlife in the Jewish Tradition

Carla Wills-Brandon, Ph.D.

Inner Traditions
Rochester, Vermont

Inner Traditions
One Park Street
Rochester, Vermont 05767
www.InnerTraditions.com

Cataloging-in-Publication Data for this title is available from the Library of Congress

ISBN 978-1-64411-815-3 (print)
ISBN 978-1-64411-816-0 (ebook)

Printed and bound in the United States by Lake Book Manufacturing, LLC

10 9 8 7 6 5 4 3 2 1

Text design and layout by Priscilla Harris Baker and Kenleigh Manseau
This book was typeset in Garamond Premier Pro with Carentro, Gill Sans, Legacy Sans, and Optima used as display typefaces

"I Saw My Grandmother's Soul Leave Her Body" by Salvador Litvak was reprinted with permission from the author. The essay can be found in its entirety at his website The Accidental Talmudist.

To send correspondence to the author of this book, mail a first-class letter to the author c/o Inner Traditions • Bear & Company, One Park Street, Rochester, VT 05767, and we will forward the communication.

Life is a tapestry; weave it well.

This book is first dedicated to Holocaust victims, those
who perished and those who survived, along with those
who died at the hands of Hitler, Lenin, and Stalin,
those who have suffered genocide or have such
atrocities in their family roots. I acknowledge
the work many in the following generations
have done to not only clean up the wreckage
of the past but also to heal into the present.
Finally, I embrace with deep love
my family—Michael, Aaron, and Josh.
Together, we can continue to practice tikkun olam.

Ein Sof

While climbing up on Jacob's ladder
I turn around to see
Those overcome with mournful sorrow,
And comfort those who still believe.
Our journey has no morrow.
"Fear not," I say,
"True love persists ne'er ending,
And over time what's seen today
Will only change its rend'ring.
And yet God's hand is at our side,
And will forever be.
"We'll ne'er be here left all alone
Despite our mortal toil.
And even though our journey home
Is filled with hoops and strings,
There's more to life and to our love
Than these confounding things.
"The path behind leads on beyond—
It's far from a nonentity.
We look ahead and heed the Guide
That leads us to infinity."

—CARLA WILLS-BRANDON

Contents

✡

Acknowledgments

I live three blocks from the ocean. Once a year we have a sandcastle competition on the beach. Ingredients needed for building a great piece of sand art include minute polished sand stones, well-defined tiny seashells, flowing ocean waters, lots of beach goers, and green, yellow, white, or chocolate colored seagrass. *Seven Heavens: The Afterlife in the Jewish Tradition* was created by many gifted castle builders.

For surrounding me with strength and wisdom, I want to express my gratitude to Ted Wills Jr., John White, Rabbi Jimmy Kessler, Rabbi Peter Kessler, Rabbi Roy Walters, Dr. Jeffrey Long, Dr. Bruce Greyson, Mark Anthony, Tikvah Feinstein, Michael Tymn, Laura Reeves, Paige Almaraz, Dr. David Ware, Laura Asadoorian Blaney, and Gail & Mary Kilgore.

Finally, and especially: to my family at Inner Traditions without whose help this would never have become a reality. I am especially grateful to Jon Graham, Jeanie Levitan, Courtney Jenkins, Emilia Cataldo, Kelly Bowen, and Ashley Kolesnik. They put the defining touches on this sandcastle.

Foreword

I was introduced to Carla Wills-Brandon, Ph.D., almost a quarter century ago through her inspiring and heartwarming book *One Last Hug before I Go,* a trailblazing exploration of deathbed visions, including dying individuals' visions and final words, survivors' mystical experiences and premonitions preceding a loved one's passing, accounts of seeing the soul leave the body, and after-death communications. She went on to write additional books on mystical experiences surrounding the transition from life to death: *Heavenly Hugs* and *A Glimpse of Heaven.* All these works draw heavily on the experiences of her clients as a licensed marriage and family therapist, on her extensive research, and on her personal experiences.

Seven Heavens breaks new ground in exploring the parallels between these contemporary spiritual experiences and evidence for life after death from ancient Jewish beliefs. Wills-Brandon uncovers references to the afterlife, to Jewish mysticism, and to spiritual encounters in a variety of ancient Hebrew texts, including the Torah, the Talmud, the Zohar, the Dead Sea Scrolls, and the writings of the early Kabbalists. These sources describe what we now recognize as near-death experiences, after-death communications, reincarnation memories, and deathbed visions of deceased loved ones. The "seven heavens" in the title refers to the concept, common to early Judaism, Christianity, Islam,

Hinduism, and Jainism, of seven levels or divisions of the heavens.

Wills-Brandon shows readers the parallels between mystical experiences we see today and to those described in the ancient texts. She traces efforts to communicate with the dead back at least five thousand years. Her research suggests that no matter how our civilization evolves in coming centuries, we will undoubtedly continue to be fascinated by people who claim to talk with the dead.

In *Seven Heavens* Wills-Brandon shares profound stories from her clinical psychotherapy practice demonstrating how afterlife beliefs can heal destructive emotional patterns. The distress from trauma can be healed through sharing spiritual experiences, even when it has been hardened by generation after generation, such as the intergeneration traumatic wounds in the children and grandchildren of Holocaust survivors with post-traumatic stress disorder. We usually associate the Holocaust and other mass evils with terrifying experiences, but survivors of such horrors also speak of incredible virtue of people around them and their gratitude for the help they received from courageous people. The saving grace for survivors of such gruesome events has been the acts of courage fellow victims and other people showed to save families, friends, fellow prisoners, and themselves. Wills-Brandon describes Holocaust survivors who were able to experience gratitude after listening to others'—or sharing their own—near-death experiences, after-death communications, and deathbed visions.

Through profound stories of her clients, friends, and family, Wills-Brandon shows that acknowledging an afterlife and mystical encounters in this life can help us find peace after loss, discover inner spiritual light, and heal from destructive emotional patterns. She argues from personal and professional experience that believing in life after death and sharing spiritual experiences can help heal emotional trauma and release painful memories. Knowing that our consciousness survives physical death promotes a healthier preparation for our own death and the deaths of our loved ones.

Despite its subtitle, *The Afterlife in Jewish Tradition, Seven Heavens* does not speak only to Jews. Wills-Brandon's research reveals that all religions are ways of rediscovering ourselves and our spiritual nature, and that afterlife communications can be found within every spiritual tradition. Many people around the world in recent decades have become disillusioned with their religions, seeking alternative spiritual traditions or giving up on religion entirely and embracing atheism. Wills-Brandon shows that every religion contains a kernel, however hidden in today's materialistic culture, of spirituality and mysticism that can lead us back to a sense of communion with fellow worshippers, with a rich tradition going back centuries and encircling the globe, and with the divine. To live our lives to the fullest, we have to outgrow the illusion that death is an ending. But as Wills-Brandon shows, these revelations, both modern and ancient, reveal not just an afterlife, but, perhaps more importantly, another life *here and now* beyond the physical.

Readers should not expect a dispassionate scientific or sociological treatise in *Seven Heavens*. This is a book written by the heart, and speaking to the heart. The question for readers is: Are you ready to entertain evidence for how fear of death blunts our spiritual evolution, and how acknowledging a life beyond bodily death can lead to personal and spiritual growth? I join Carla Wills-Brandon in encouraging you to open your heart and mind and give yourself a chance.

BRUCE GREYSON, M.D.,
CHARLOTTESVILLE, VIRGINIA,
MARCH 14, 2023

BRUCE GREYSON, M.D., is professor emeritus of psychiatry and neurobehavioral sciences at the University of Virginia, and author of *After: A Doctor Explores What Near-Death Experiences Reveal about Life and Beyond.*

Why Seven Heavens?

Woe is us! The world is full of light and mysteries both wonderful and awesome, but our tiny little hand shades our eyes and prevents them from seeing.

—RABBI NACHMAN OF BRESLOV

While reading the Torah, a very important ancient Judaic text, I discovered there were seven heavens or seven levels or divisions of heaven that made up the one heaven. Wondering why there were so many heavens, I found myself worrying over which heaven I would go to.

Digging deeper, I found this belief was present within other religions and spiritual philosophies. In Islam there are also seven levels of heaven, the highest being the seventh, Dar-us Salam, the abode of well-being.

Before looking more closely at Judaism, I'd discovered there were several parallels between Christianity and Islam. Jesus turned water into wine for a multitude of wedding guests, and Muhammad put a small amount of water in his hand and then a copious amount flowed through his fingers, quenching the thirst of his followers. Miracles did happen.

Despite the connections among and similarities of the three Abrahamic religions, there has been much enmity among them through the millennia. Those opposing religions they did not subscribe to had little regard for the leaders of those religions and were quick to plot assassinations and torture, imprison, and murder religious followers and leaders. Islam and the prophet Muhammad or Mahomet has gotten rough treatment from Christians. But there has been something of a reassessment, which started with Scottish essayist Thomas Carlyle, who wrote in the middle of the nineteenth century:

> Our current hypothesis about Mahomet, that he was a scheming Imposter, a Falsehood incarnate, that his religion is a mere mass of quackery and fatuity, begins really to be now untenable to anyone. The lies, which well-meaning zeal has heaped round this man, are disgraceful to us only.

That's a rough review.

Then there's Moses, the leader of the Israelites. Moses had a bad temper. Anger and raging were methods for dealing with his frustrations. He experienced several unusual near-death experiences, among them the burning bush at Mount Sinai where he met God. After Moses met God, he was able to use these emotions and lead the Israelites out of Egypt. His physical body did not feel the burning flame of God. According to history this was the first time God had ever talked to anyone.

> *And the Angel of the Lord appeared unto him in a flame*
> *of light out in the midst of a bush: and he looked and*
> *behold, the bush burned with fire and behold, the bush*
> *was not consumed.*
>
> —EXODUS 3:3

Unfortunately, though he didn't burn physically, he had a temper that could incinerate his followers. His intense rage was over the top. It was unthinkable that a man such as Moses show this kind of anger in the presence of the entire community. As Rabbi Susan Leider remarks in her article "When Moses Boils Over, We Take Stock of Our Own Anger": "You can almost hear Maimonides* saying, 'What a shanda. What a shame that we should see a leader behave like this.'"

Was this rage because of disappointment, fear, anger, frustration, or irritation? Does it seem like appropriate anger, proper for the time? Or did it emanate from an impulse to run or hide away, or from self-destructiveness and self-hate?

Though frustrated with the Israelites, Moses's fury may have saved the lives of his chaotic wandering flock. He used his rage to move them into action, and because of this, they were no longer lost in pandemonium.

FINALLY, A FOUNDATION

This gave me a beginning in understanding monolithic ideas of God and war. The seven heavens, many ethereal destinations and houses found within heaven and religion helped me begin to see the language of the afterlife.

These ancient people and their beliefs fostered offshoots of other religions. All of this had to have started somewhere. Like it or not I knew I would never have all the answers, but that didn't mean I couldn't keep exploring.

Also, I had to accept that even powerful men can become rageful, but still do good in the world. This took the pressure off me. I didn't need to be perfect. I could channel my anger into a more productive power, which would help me and others.

Watching popular modern Christian movements, I realized many current followers didn't know the man named Jesus was a Jew. He had a Jewish upbringing, with Jewish parents, siblings, and relatives

---

*Moses ben Maimon, also known as Rambam, Spanish Jewish philosopher (1138-1204).

within a very Jewish community. I've even seen Jesus depicted in art wearing a tallit, or Jewish prayer shawl. He was a Jew and practiced the Jewish religion. Being a Jew, he would have followed those Jewish laws pertaining to the prayer shawl. During debates about Jesus the Jew, I've had religious books with evidence sitting in front of me and been told I didn't know what I was talking about.

We know Jesus was angry at the Pharisees who were constantly working at scheming his murder. As Sam O'Neal notes in his article "The Difference between Pharisees and Sadducees in the Bible:" "To put things simply, the Pharisees believed in the supernatural—angels, demons, heaven, hell and so on—while the Sadducees did not." They also, unlike the Sadducees, believed in an afterlife. The Pharisees were a Jewish social movement of mostly middle-class businessmen, while the Sadducees were a powerful Jewish socioreligious sect of high priests and aristocratic families. Though Jesus raged at the Pharisees, it was the Saducees who ultimately rejected him and supported his crucifixion.

He was also very rageful at his good friend Lazarus. He yelled at him and told him to come out of his grave. Supposedly Lazarus did what Jesus said and rose out of his burial place. Spiritually speaking, both of these religious leaders had afterlife experiences.

JEWS AND BELIEF IN THE AFTERLIFE

Often I'm asked: "Do Jews believe in life after death? Is there some part of us that never dies?" I respond that I've researched and written three books on the afterlife encounters the dying have reported just before physical death occurs. What I've discovered is that, like most cultures around the world, we Jews also have these experiences. Within ancient writings we find examples of this phenomena. Unfortunately, past traumas in Judaic history have put a damper on our confidence in anything not completely explainable. By shading our eyes, we will never be able to see the whole picture. To understand Jewish afterlife experiences, we will need time to fully explore this question. Then we must meditate on what we've learned. It doesn't matter if we are believers, agnostics, or atheists. The journey is progressive, one step at a time and all of us can learn from the journey.

The Sabbath is a twinkling in time for reflection and contemplation. We don't necessarily need to be religious for such consideration, but with quiet time we see where we've come from and then prepare for the future. We can also ask ourselves what inner work we must do to become more internally fit and at peace with ourselves. This sacred space gives us a moment to rest and take stock of ourselves without distraction. In doing this regularly, we begin to have moments of enlightenment. With new awareness or insight, we become more open to new ideas, experiences, and awe-inspiring flashes of illumination.

To begin this process of discovering who we really are, we need to treat our journey as an enlightened Sabbath. Only in this way can we make room for the light or balanced understanding of the inner self. The darkness of hidden pain can block us from knowing who we truly are. Believing the trauma of our ancestors never impacted us can be one way we shut ourselves off from a world that has so much to offer. Quiet time can help us release difficult emotions and memories stuck psychically in our past.

No matter which sect of Judaism one practices, there is a commonality. This may be the recognition of order in the universe. Some people call it God, consciousness, creativity, or that shard of inner light within each of us, which comes from a much bigger source.

Unresolved pain can make it difficult for us to see or experience our natural spirituality. The unresolved free-floating or unexplained feelings of grief, fear, depression, shame, and even numbness can hinder our journey. Sadly, this can also manifest as unexplained anxiety, relationship issues, anger, low self-esteem or sense of self-worth, an inability to trust, and even addiction. For many families post-traumatic stress disorder or PTSD can create a great deal of distress in the family system.

The Holocaust created enormous PTSD for many survivors. Then there can be a trickledown effect, where feelings about this gruesome time are passed on down from one generation to the next. Descendants need not have experienced firsthand trauma, concentration camps, imprisonment in gulags, or starvation. The secrets of this period were and continue to be kept by many survivors. Because of this, the following generations became at risk for carrying feelings related to losses and traumas they never were part of.

Because of this, many Jews are secular or only traditionally cultural, without putting trust in any form of a universal order. As the writer and artist Lesli Koppelman Ross wrote in her book about Jewish holidays, concerning the meaning of Yom Hashoah: "To spare their descendants the horrors they had endured, they abandoned Judaism, converted to another religion, or raised their children as non-Jews."

When tragedy happens to us or our loved ones, we can't just bury the event. To have a completely fulfilling life and sense of well-being, a series of progressive steps must be taken. Grief, loss, and secrets are often the biggest of obstacles. Taking the time to honestly reflect on the sadness and traumas we or our families have had to endure will have its rewards. Being aware and interested in those spiritual experiences we once brushed aside opens us up to more possibilities.

Understand this is not about blaming our loved ones. When my grandfather didn't speak and instead kept secrets, he thought he was protecting me. Reflection on family secrets or sad events frees us up from those emotions we've never understood. When we do this, the sweetness of life will become even more fragrant.

INTRODUCTION

Secrets We Keep

I don't speak because I have the power to speak; I speak because I don't have the power to remain silent.

—RABBI ABRAHAM ISAAC KOOK

Prolific writer J. R. Barrett, author of more than thirty books, had a profound near-death experience when, during a horseback ride, her horse threw her.

Her parents and other family members were Holocaust survivors with harrowing memories. Barrett's father, with French and Romanian Ashkenazi roots, was a child during World War II and never recovered from his anger toward the Nazis. An atheist, he worked as a lawyer for a horse owner. Barrett's uncle, her father's oldest brother, was in a German POW camp during World War II. Barrett says his experiences were extremely heartbreaking. Barrett's mother, a Swedish Sephardic Jew and an agnostic, had departing visions on her deathbed.

Before Barrett's near-death event, she reported that "the sky was golden bright, and the wind was blustery." She was astride her horse on a ridge when she saw a man riding an Arabian horse, screaming as he galloped down the hill. Her horse responded by rearing up.

1

Sitting in the Lap of Good
J. R. Barrett

My horse reared up and flipped over me. He then reared up again a second time with his feet skidding on the downhill side.

I left my body, [with] no care about my body. I saw [my] sisters putting their hands over their faces. Then I felt someone on my left, "come with me". . . a three-dimensional hand came forward. . . . Holding hands, and surfing. Before I hit the barrier, I could differentiate. Hitting the barrier, I saw we were all connected. . . . Next, I saw a warm light, but it didn't hurt my eyes. It felt like I was sitting in the lap of good. A face was buried into this light. He pulled a part of himself away. Far away I could see every blade of grass, every flower. People were coming through the meadow. The guy [with the three-dimensional hand] said, "You have to go back." I said, "No." I had a panic attack. I was slammed back into my body. Charlie, the guy who owned the ranch, threw me across the horse and took me to get help for a broken pelvis and broken lower back.

The message she received was: "All paths lead to God. All paths lead to truth."

THE NO-TALK RULE

In this book are numerous accounts like that of J. R. Barrett of near-death experiences and of contacts with the deceased and departing visions from dying loved ones. Hopefully, these stories will show that Jews too have life-after-death experiences. Currently, there is a widespread belief that Jews don't believe in an afterlife. How can this perception be true? Why have our near-death experiences, afterlife communications, dreams about deceased relatives, premonitions of things to come, or contact with those in spirit been ignored? Who made this rule, and how did it come to be?

I know there are many individuals, including those who are Jewish, who've had encounters with some sort of afterlife. How do I know this? For over thirty years I've investigated at least two thousand events from around the world. These experiences can be found in every religion and tradition, including Judaism. When I speak of Judaism, I'm including all branches of Judaism, those born Jewish or who have converted, along with practicing and secular Jews.

Though I've come across numerous Jewish experiencers, I've seen very few books discussing this phenomenon. I've also discovered within the Jewish community, personal life-after-death experiences are rarely shared openly. Why is this? I believe it has a lot to do with an unconsciously instilled no-talk rule. The no-talk rule exists in every culture, but when it comes to today's modern Judaism, these incredible encounters are often shunned. Sadly, over the last decades, this unspoken rule has only grown stronger.

People who have these experiences usually turn to me first to discuss their encounter, rather than share it with other members of their Jewish community, including their rabbi. Those who are thinking of talking with me will first check me out very carefully. Questions tossed my way include: "How long have you been in private clinical practice?" "What is your highest degree of education?" "How many books have you written?" And the most reasonable of all questions: "Why should I trust you?" I always let people know they don't have to trust me and that I'm just a sounding board with information. If they want to talk, I hear them out. Then I discuss with them what research has been done on near-death experiences and my special area of interest, the departing visions of the dying.

Departing visions or, as they have been previously called, deathbed visions can be found in every ethnic and cultural group. Throughout the centuries, there have been many documented cases of people witnessing a dying loved one talk with relatives or friends who have preceded them in death. These conversations between our dying loved ones and those we cannot see are precious to the experiencer. There is a sense of joy in reuniting with these individuals. For the physically dying person, having a departing vision causes all concerns about death and dying to evaporate. Research has also shown that a once combative patient will suddenly become pleasant and calm after the experience. Then there are those of us who aren't passing. Our loved one who is dying or has already passed may visit us in our dreams or in spirit form. They come to us to let us know they will be fine, they love us, or to leave us with some other message.

In a hospital, miles away from our family home, my mother was preparing to pass. At the exact moment of her physical death, I knew she had moved on. There was a strong knowing that her physical end had occurred. The phone rang shortly after she had left her weary body. It was a friend of hers from the hospital. He let me know my mother had just died. Did I have anyone to talk to about my departing visitation from my mother? The answer is no. Like many, I remained silent, and there is a reason for this. Countless families have lived by the no-talk rule, which has been passed on down from one generation to the next. Consciously or unconsciously, this behavior has made its way from great-grandparents, to grandparents, to parents, and finally to us. We learned early on that afterlife encounters were one of many secrets we shouldn't discuss.

My Encounter with the Afterlife

For years I kept silent about my own near-death experience, when I almost died because of a calcium overload. I have Crohn's disease (an autoimmune disorder) and was told to increase my calcium. Well, I thought more was better. About six months before being hospitalized, I had a flare-up. The calcium I'd been taking for years had been removed from the market. In its place I grabbed a run-of-the-mill over-the-counter calcium. Big mistake. And no, I didn't read that "follow directions" phrase on the back of the bottle.

Over time I started having memory loss and muscle problems. In a few months, lethargy had set in, and I began finding it hard to stay awake. I thought maybe I had mononucleosis or the flu. Long story short, I started to lose consciousness. My oldest son and husband put me in the car and took me to my doctor. My calcium levels were off the charts. My doctor wondered how I was still alive. Immediately, I found myself in the hospital. The specialist who was also an astronaut finally figured out the problem. Good thing he hadn't been flying in space that day.

I remember little of those first few hours or even days but did recall a profound experience. First, I was hospitalized in the exact same room my father-in-law had been in before he died. Second, I remember being in the bed when suddenly a very, very bright golden light appeared.

Then I heard music. There was someone, a holy man of sorts, leading prayers for groups of people separated from me. Listening to this, I felt joy and peace. The sensations of warmth, safety, and calmness surrounded me physically, emotionally, and spiritually. As the holy man continued to speak, the tinkling of bells and chimes lingered. Those in the groups were moving around, visiting and enjoying themselves. It was like being at a party I wasn't invited to.

There were no windows in my room, either opening out to the outside or to the hallway. It would have been impossible for a bright light to have filtered into my room, which I later discovered was adjacent to a dim-lit nurses' desk. Later, I had my husband check to see if someone had been listening to music on a radio somewhere near my room; there was no radio. After the fact I even checked my medical chart to see if I had been on any strong medications. The answer was no: potassium was the only medication I was given.

The day before this life-threatening event I'd been very frightened. I even tried to escape the hospital. After the illness I was also told I had been talking like a nut.

There were no tunnels to heaven, only the sensation of floating, a calming golden light, golden human-like forms, tinkling music, and soothing words from a spiritual being. And I was conscious during the whole experience. In real time I saw souls who seemed as human as you or I. Years ago I was told by a mentor that those living on the other side can appear to us as they were in physical life. Also, they can speak as they did when living in this world. Any funny quirks they had while alive in the material world will follow these spirits into an afterlife existence. For me this was an amazing experience. But when I recovered, did many of my peers want to hear about this? Maybe a few, but for the most part, no—for years I kept silent.

FAMILY SECRETS

I do know about secrets because I was born in a family with a closet full of skeletons. Dark secrets about persecution and loss of dignity were whispered in back rooms. Most of this history would be hidden from me for many years. Even when I was older, my grandparents and great-grandparents would never really share all of their history, or how relatives had been left behind in Russia—shot, starved, hung, or sent to the gulags or deadly concentration camps in Siberia. The belief was this secrecy was in the family's best interest. Today, I feel the generations before me believed in what they were doing. Yes, rule number one was in play, and it went something like this: "We don't talk about things that are uncomfortable, frightening, or grief provoking. We must protect the children and ourselves from feelings and memories related to the past."

Regardless of this very flawed, deep-rooted code, publicly my family appeared to be just like everyone else's. Living in an ethnic community, we thought our family's ups and downs were just like everyone else's. As a clinician, I eventually recognized my family was far from normal. I began to remember how older relatives would go into back rooms to talk, speaking in languages I didn't understand. When they were with me, my siblings, or my cousins, conversation would be whispered with a hand over the lips to make sure we couldn't see or hear what they were discussing. Speaking Russian or a very old-school German, along with bits of Polish and Yiddish, kept my generation in the dark.

In middle school all of us in our grade learned German. As a young girl clothed in modest dresses made by my grandmother, I remember sitting in class with the teacher instructing us on how to speak this old form of German. In high school I tried to understand the language of my elders by taking modern-day German. Sadly, I quickly I discovered this was not the tongue I'd heard in my family.

Growing up with the same foods and customs as many of my schoolmates seemed normal. When I went to lunch at my elementary school, those same ethnic foods were often served in the cafeteria. At big gatherings, I didn't realize everyone present was related to me. Shopping with my grandmother for food, clothing, or a root beer float always took place at small shops. As the shopkeepers and my grandmother spoke in English, smattered with other languages, I was impatient to go to lunch for a *bierock,* which is like a pierogi, and to the bakery for apricot kuchen, a type of cake. Little did I know we always received a good deal or no charge because the owner was a family member who had also escaped the misfortunes of Russia.

These relatives and friends had come from small villages or shtetls in Russia. Older women in long black dresses with hair tightly wound into a bun at the nape of the neck were the norm. Wearing brightly colored shawls wrapped around their shoulders, they would make sure the younger generation would eat everything on their plates. Looking back, even the tobacco pipes a few of the men smoked looked unique.

Yearning for a new life, one which wasn't ruled by terror and bleakness, my great-grandparents, grandparents, and uncles and aunts tried to erase their tragic history. Though religious, devoted to family, and hardworking, the past still haunted them. In their own homeland, they had become the enemy. With this, the once-sheltered remembrance of living with pride in Russia had been shattered. What would it be like in America? To answer the question and make this work, the past had to be buried. Here we have the birth of a "no-talk rule."

RUSSIA'S RUGGED HISTORY OF ANTI-SEMITISM

The anti-Jewish pogroms of the early nineteenth century followed by the Russian Revolution of January 22, 1905 (Bloody Sunday); trips to the gulags in Siberia, first instituted by Lenin and continued by Stalin; and the man-made famines created by the Kremlin in 1932–1933 all inflicted waves of terror on Russia's, and later the Soviet Union's, Jewish population. Formerly semi-acceptable political leaders vanished, while ruthless tyrants slid into seats of power.

The first dictator of the Marxist state, Bolshevik leader Vladimir Lenin (1870–1924), grew up with many secrets. For one, his mother, Maria Alexandrovna Ulyanova Blank (1835–1916), was ethnically tied to groups in Russia like mine. Lenin's mother's father, Alexander Blank (born Srul Israel Blank), was a well-to-do physician who was Jewish by birth but converted to Orthodox Christianity in adulthood. This was necessary to improve his status in the professional world. Living in Russia during the Tsarist period as a Jew opened one up to a great deal of dangerous discrimination. Looking at Lenin's politics, I believe his fight against anti-Semitism had a lot to do with his mother's background. Lenin, along with Tolstoy, condemned the pogroms. In 1914 Lenin and the Bolsheviks submitted a bill stating that all laws restricting Jews in all areas of life be abolished. He saw anti-Semitism as contrary to the fundamental socialist tenet of equality. Though Lenin did not target Jews, the Bolsheviks unleashed a reign of terror, known as the Red Terror, after an assassination attempt on Lenin in 1918. Tens of thousands were arrested, interrogated, tortured, sent to labor camps, and executed, among them Christian clergy, non-Bolshevik socialists, foreigners, and many others seen as enemies of the Soviet state.

When Lenin died in 1924, Joseph Stalin (1878–1953), a more brutal warlord, took over. Stalin's parents came from Orthodox Christian serf families. His father had a severe drinking problem, which not only affected his work, but also made him very abusive toward his family. Once in power Stalin wanted to change Russia into an industrial society. In doing so, he and his government are accountable for hundreds of thousands of executions, along with millions of deaths resulting from politically induced starvations and hard labor camps. This madman's forced industrialization created the worst man-made famine in history.

Relatives perished during this time, but the family never talked of this. Instead, food was of most importance. If younger people wasted food, our elders would give us a look or make a comment. They or their loved ones had starved, so was it a surprise that they used food or lack of it to bind our emotions?

While living with my grandparents in the 1970s, I heard something that gave me an intense sick feeling. That strong emotion was survivor's guilt. I discovered there were relatives still living in miserable conditions in Russia. My grandparents and other relatives were making attempts to send them goods and offer help. I felt powerless and ashamed and wondered what I could do to aid these loved ones. They had the same blood running through their veins as I did. During this time, I heard my elders say, "Where is God in all this?" Angrily, I too asked this same question.

As I grew older, I'd ask my grandfather about family history. Intuition told me he knew all the family secrets. Holding my hands in his, he would say, "Forget the past. Look only toward the future. Be proud you're an American living in America."

Like many immigrants, my family came to this country with the shirts on their backs and a few rubles in their pockets. Immediately they went to work as laborers. My grandmother was a housekeeper for a Jewish family who had already settled in the area years before. The first and second generations seldom married outside of the ethnic group. I was set up to marry a cousin. Americanization and the ability to speak English as soon as possible was a must. Older family members did not want me, my siblings, or cousins to ever live the lives they had endured back in Russia.

When I left home, I was still walking around with old-world traditions that had been drilled into me. This involved everything from how I dressed, my values, and even how I cooked. Also instilled in me was distrust. My history was a secret. Not talking about anything unpleasant was just the way it was. My family believed living safely in America meant leaving all notions of the old country, with its traumas and losses, behind. This included my natural sense of spirituality.

I eventually did my family of origin work, drawing family trees, and airing out the skeletons in the family closet. I learned what my relatives had really endured in Russia and the United States. Then, I looked at how these traumas had impacted me. Getting honest about where I came from showed me why the secrets had developed in our family. In doing this the hidden mysteries were hidden no more. With this my natural sense of spirituality began to blossom. I finally felt free to look at my departing visions with my mother before she passed and see these incredible events for what they really were. It was spiritual and special. Before this, all I had known was their feelings and my twisted resentments. Finally, it was time to use these departing visions as a starting point for looking into other afterlife experiences already documented.

This also prepared me for those afterlife encounters to come. Today, my life is not only about embracing my once lost history but also about listening to the afterlife accounts of others. The journey has been totally worth it, and now I'd like to pass on to you some of the information I've collected.

ONE

Where to Start

Focusing too hard on our differences can trip us up!

—CARLA WILLS-BRANDON

In the beginning, God created the heavens and the earth.

—GENESIS 1:1

The quoted passage from Genesis has puzzled me for years. Where did the beginning start? Who was the Creator? And what came before the creation? Who is responsible for the birth of the Creator and why did creation need to happen? Finally, who is God, and what is heaven?

I've talked to many people from different parts of the world who emphatically believe Judaism is the first real religion. This couldn't be further from the truth. If one takes the time to investigate religion and spiritual philosophy, it will become evident that there were a multitude of ideas before the birth of Judaism. Also, many other religions believe they are the first and only religion.

Unbeknown to present and past seekers, many religions date some time back. Some of the oldest religions were formed before Judaism. Hinduism is considered by some to be the world's most ancient extant religion, dating back over four thousand years ago. Many branches of Hinduism believe in one God, but some embrace multiple gods and goddesses. Another ancient religion, predating Judaism, is Zoroastrianism.

LANGUAGES AND HUMAN HISTORY: THE HEBREW LANGUAGE

According to Allen P. Ross, professor of divinity at Beeson Divinity School, in his book *Introducing Biblical Hebrew* "Hebrew belongs to the Canaanite group. Canaanite languages are a branch of the Northwest Semitic family of languages." Ross tells us Hebrew was and is a language made up of a group of languages. With the modern Hebrew language, we ask, is this based on the history of the ages or some sort of modern-day Hebrew? And is this modern-day dialect an original language?

Between the tenth and sixth century BCE, another form of this ever-evolving language surfaced. The Monarchical Period in Israel (1050–920 BCE) produced a language rooted in the ancient Hebrew language of the Israelite Samaritans. This form of the language can be seen in the Tanakh, a collection of Hebrew scriptures that includes the Torah, the Nevi'im, and the Ketuvim; the word *Tanakh* is an acronym derived from these three divisions of the Hebrew Bible. Looking at the writing used in putting together the Torah, we can determine during which era a body of work was produced. For example, if we study just a few ancient documents, we might see crowns sitting on top of certain Hebrew script characters. This style of writing tells us it was created during the Monarchical Period. The royal crowns topping the script gives us a time in history. With investigation we can learn who the royals of the time were and what their politics and private lives looked like. We also get a glimpse of what was going on during this time in history.

The United Monarchy is the name given to the united Israelite kingdom of Israel and Judah during the reigns of Saul, David, and Solomon, as depicted in the Hebrew Bible. It is traditionally dated to have lasted from 1047 BCE to 930 BCE. We can see how Hebrew changed from one century to the next. Investigators must continue to look at languages with their different dialects and meanings.

No matter how far back we go in history, there is evidence of a human desire to dissect languages. We are all searching for different meanings and clues. It doesn't matter what tongue we speak, job we have, religion or philosophy we resonate with. If we can't understand this, how are we going to understand afterlife language? One word may mean something to a man in Egypt and another to a child in Israel.

COMMUNICATING WITH THE DEAD AND PRECOGNITION

Trying to commune with the dead, or predict the future, can be traced back at least five thousand years. Fortune telling, the prediction of events to come, or having uncommon abilities like contact with those who have passed on, are not considered to have a rational basis. The ancient Egyptians practiced scrying or reading shapes formed in water by dropping ink into liquid. The Mesopotamians did the same thing but with oil. Palmistry is believed to have originated in India. When a Chinese emperor discovered tea in 2737 BCE, his followers began reading tea leaves.

The Torah and the Bible act as prediction manuals. One of the most famous forecasters of things to come was Nostradamus (1503–1566), a sixteenth-century French astrologer. His work *The Prophecies* is a famous manuscript containing international prophecies for the coming times.

Also, by the 1700s, the French had turned tarot playing cards, created in the 1440s, into a tool of prophecy. Then there are the Victorians.

The era started in the early 1800s. Victorians were fascinated with speaking to the dead through a medium—a person who claims to be able to speak to the dead or spirits. And, in the first decades of the 1900s, the mystic Rasputin captured Russian imaginations.

No matter how civilization continues to evolve, our fascination with people who claim to tell us what our futures are, or those who talk to the dead, continues. Modern-day television has capitalized on this for years. Whether you believe in their line of work or not, there's a good chance that two hundred years from now, psychics and mediums will still be just as in demand as they are today.

Holocaust Survivors and Gratitude

In 2015 neuroscientist Glenn R. Fox, along with three coauthors, published a research article on the neurobiological correlates of gratitude called "Neural Correlates of Gratitude" (*Frontiers in Psychology*). They wanted to elucidate the neurology of gratitude, hypothesizing that it would correlate with regions of the brain associated with moral cognition and value judgment.

To elicit gratitude in their test subjects, they used the stories of Holocaust survivors, who had been sheltered by strangers and received food and clothing. The researchers analyzed audio recordings from the USC Shoah Foundation and used this information to design their brain-scan study.

"When they gave testimony to USC Shoah Foundation many Holocaust survivors told us that they found a reason to be grateful, whether it was because of a stranger offering a bit of food or a neighbor providing a place to hide," said Dr. Stephen Smith, USC Shoah Foundation executive director. "These small acts of generosity helped them hold on to their humanity. That Glenn has been able to use testimonies in his incredible research on gratitude shows why it is so important to preserve the voices of people who lived through these dark times."

The twenty-three participants (half men, half women) had no connection to the Holocaust. They were shown documentaries about the Holocaust, and also images of concentration camp victims being liberated. They were asked to imagine themselves in the context of the Holocaust and how they would respond if they received lifesaving gifts of shelter, food, and clothing. When they responded to a prompt—such as, "You have been sick for weeks. A prisoner who is a doctor finds medicine and saves your life"—the researchers monitored the participants' brain activity, using MRI scans. The results confirmed their hypothesis. When subjects felt gratitude, areas of the brain responsible for feelings of reward, fairness, moral cognition, and value judgments, among others, were activated.

In an interview, Fox observed, "In the midst of this awful tragedy, there were many acts of bravery and lifesaving aid. With the Holocaust, we typically only associate the awful things. But when you listen to the survivors, you also hear stories of incredible virtue, and gratitude for the help they received."

In my research I have found Holocaust survivors who were able to experience gratitude after hearing or sharing deathbed visions, near-death experiences, premonition of things to come, and after-death communications.

Did our spiritual quest start with Hinduism, the Pharisees, Islam, Buddhism, the Sadducees, or Judaism? As we have seen the answer is no. There are numerous belief systems out there. Though many people wrongly believe Judaism is the oldest religion, this is far from the truth. One religion birthed another. The belief in one God, supreme being, or psychic force dates to at least a number of millenniums ago. When I share this with seekers, typical reactions are disappointment or anger, followed with, "Oh, what do you know? Where is your degree in ancient religious history?"

Religion and philosophy are humanity's way of continually discovering itself and the world in which we live. Afterlife contact can be found within every spiritual pursuit, and Judaism is no different. We need to recognize Judaism has a rich history with the world to come. The following chapters will be devoted to clearing up the past and looking at Judaism's rich relationship with the afterlife.

TWO

The Afterlife in the Jewish Tradition

This world is like a lobby before Olam Ha-Ba. Prepare yourself in the lobby so that you may enter the banquet hall.

—RABBI YAAKOV, PIRKEI AVOT 4:16

In our modern culture many Jews and non-Jews alike believe the afterlife holds no place in Judaism. As a Jew, I'm very aware that belief in an afterlife is not popular. Modern-day Judaism tends to push such matters aside, emphasizing living a good life in the here and now, doing *mitzvot* (good deeds), and caring for those around us. This is where much of our attention should be. Unlike many other world religions, Judaism places great importance on leaving this world a better place by addressing issues concerning humanity and the health of the planet.

Because Judaism emphasizes the here and now, few Jews are aware that it has a rich tradition of belief in a world to come. I have heard time and again that Judaism has no interest in contact with an afterlife or world to come. This couldn't be further from the truth. All one needs to do is explore not only the Torah or Talmud but also other earlier historical writings. As Rabbi Baruch HaLevi so eloquently said, in an article for Jewish Boston: "*Jews* may not believe in the afterlife—heaven and hell—but *Judaism* unequivocally does."

LOOKING BACKWARD
TO UNDERSTAND TODAY

Years ago I was privileged to see the Dead Sea Scrolls. Found in 1947 by a Bedouin boy looking for a lost animal, the over two-thousand-year-old writings were discovered in a cave enclosed in clay jars. The fragile sheets of papyrus were found near the settlement of Qumran, located in the Judean Desert of the West Bank. They were eventually shown to a high member of the Syriac Orthodox Church of Antioch. The rest, shall we say, is history.

Much drama has followed the unearthing of these ancient fragments, so imagine my amazement at first setting my eyes on them. Reviewing the translations of Hebrew on papyrus, references to Jewish mysticism caught my attention. The scrolls provided me with a peek into ancient history and how Jews living several millenniums ago might have viewed an afterlife. Having documented and published anecdotes about the afterlife, all of which contained examples of Jewish experiences, I saw similar accounts within the scrolls. There were consistent themes describing near-death experiences, after-death contact, and departing visions. The modern-day experiences and those accounts from antiquity were very similar. After seeing the scrolls, my next question was: Why isn't there more information available on ancient afterlife accounts? If such encounters occurred so many centuries ago, and continue to happen for Jews to this day, why are so very few of us talking about them?

I'd try repeatedly to crack open the mysteries of the next life in Judaism. After a while I had to stop listening to this sort of negative banter. For many years I had listened to this and then thrown my hands up in the air saying why bother. When I quit trying so hard, I suddenly began crossing paths with rabbis and teachers who were very interested in life-after-death experiences. With their encouragement, I found myself exploring one Jewish account after another, such as deathbed visions, near-death experiences, and after-death communications. In doing this I discovered a couple of things. Each new generation of men and women with religious letters, degrees, and learning has put its own spin on these experiences. But that's not what's important. What's more significant is that the information about these experiences is available, and after much exploration and research, I have found many wonderful accounts. The problem today with modern Judaism is the lack of interest in investigating the available incredible examples of historical information about life-after-death beliefs within Jewish antiquity.

I wish I could share with you all the information that I have on this topic. But I can't. This would require several books, each five hundred pages long. Just know that it's there. Also understand that these accounts within the Jewish tradition are much like those of people from all around the world today. As we will see, it's not a new phenomenon and is not found in only one religion.

Sometimes we Jews do take things a bit too seriously. Either we work hard at Torah study, trying to be the best Jew we can be, or after the matzo ball soup, we've had enough and quietly sneak out the door. But I have a surprise for you. There is no heaven or hell. We all go to the same place when we die, where Moses and Rabbi Akiva give never-ending classes, lectures, and homework assignments on the Hebrew Bible and the Talmud. For the super righteous, this is eternal bliss, and for those of us who are not quite so upright, this can be eternal suffering.

I'm joking, of course, but the point is: there are many diverse types of Jews with different ideas about an afterlife. We all look at Judaism differently. While researching this work I found another truism about Judaism: most of us look at the idea of an afterlife or no life after death through different lenses. How many of us are aware that afterlife contact between the world we see and those who have passed was being shared orally or documented before the birth of Jesus? Saying this validates that afterlife contact is not only a religion experience. Let's look at ancient Jewish afterlife contacts.

EARLY NEAR-DEATH EXPERIENCES
AND VISIONS

Rav Huna (216–297 CE), son of Rav Yehoshua, was a very well-known Jewish Talmudist or expert in the Jewish study of the Talmud. He lived in Babylonia and was the head of an academy of learning.

The Talmud relates that around 297 CE, Rav Huna became ill. His friend Rav Pappa, also a Babylonian rabbi and master beer brewer (good combination!), went to his home to inquire about his well-being. He saw that Rav Huna was growing weak and seemed to be dying. According to the Rosh Hashanah 17a:15 (from the William Davidson Talmud digital edition), the following happened:

> Rav Pappa said to his attendants: Prepare his provisions [*zavdata*], i.e., his shrouds. In the end, Rav Huna recovered, and Rav Pappa was embarrassed to go and see him, as it seemed as if he had decreed Rav Huna's death. Rav Huna's friends said to him: What did you see when you were lying there suspended between life and death? He said to them: Yes, it was so, I was truly close to dying, but the Holy One, Blessed, be He, said to the heavenly court: Since he does not stand on his rights, i.e., he is ready to waive what is due him, you too should not be exacting with him in his judgment, as it is stated: "He bears [*noseh*] sin and forgives transgression." Whose sins does he bear? The sins of one who forgoes his reckonings with others for injustices committed against him.

After reading this, I thought to myself, "I've got a ways to go before I'm like Rav Huna!"

Here is another interesting departing vision that dates to around 90 CE. Rabban Yoḥanan ben Zakkai (30–90 CE) was Rabbi Eliezer ben Hurcanus's mentor and head of a great Yeshiva in Jerusalem. Rabbi Eliezer shared his teacher's deathbed vision experience (Berakhot 28a-b):

> At the time of his death, immediately beforehand, he said to them: Remove the vessels from the house and take them outside due to the ritual impurity that will be imparted by my corpse, which they would otherwise contract. And prepare a chair for Hezekiah, the King of Judea [739–687 BCE], who is coming from the upper world to accompany me.

It is not uncommon for the dying to report visions of religious individuals to show up to escort the dying to the next world. If you don't think that is food for thought, look at the next example.

Centuries before any of us were born, an incredible Jewish near-death experience took place, concerning Rabbi Joseph, the son of the famous Rabbi Joshua ben Levi, who lived in the first half of the third century CE. In this Talmudic near-death experience (Pesachim 50a:6), the world to come most likely implies an afterlife existence (William Davidson Talmud digital edition).

> Rav Yosef, son of Rabbi Yehoshua ben Levi, . . . became ill and was about to expire. When he returned to good health, his father said to him: What did you see when you were about to die? He said to him: I saw an inverted world. Those above, i.e., those who are considered important in this world, were below, insignificant, while those below, i.e., those who were insignificant in this world, were above. He said to him: My son, you have seen a clear world. The world you have seen is the true world, as in that world people's standings befit them.

With this near-death experience, we understand the son had seen what type of world we are trying to create, a heaven on Earth. The message in this is *tikkun olam,* which means "heal the world."

At the time I read this, I'd been very sick and stuck in difficulty. This message from across the centuries was telling me to get out of the problem and into the solution. Every time I think I've had a unique afterlife contact, I look back to history; often I discover Jews living centuries before me had already visited places like this.

HEAVENLY ACADEMIES

Years ago, I had an interesting dream. I found myself standing in a very long line of people. Everyone was chatting away, and they seemed incredibly excited. But wouldn't you know it? Here are all these happy joyous people, and I'm at the end of the line. The large group of people moved slowly into this tall, majestic building. It looked like some sort of sanctuary, and the spire on top was a million miles high. It was white in color and seemed to sparkle. As the line moved through incredibly beautiful tall doors, my neck hurt as I tried to look at the very top. Finally, the end of the line was about to enter the building. I was just about to go through the doors when I was told I needed to go back: I wasn't supposed to be there. To be honest with you, I felt extremely hurt. I wanted to be with all the happy people. What was this sanctuary about and why had I even been in the line in the first place, just to be rejected? I woke up crying and cried for several days, and then finally, I thought to myself, "You know I'm probably not supposed to leave right now because there is something more for me to do."

A few years after that, I had another dream where I was inside a similar building with all the occupants dressed in white. Again, there was a lot of white marble, and I remember thinking to myself, "This place could sure use some color." There were books everywhere, and I appeared to be in a school of some sort. Part of the building was dedicated to one type of learning, while another was devoted to other sources of learning. I spent my time wandering around but never found a way out. I knew I was here for a reason but wasn't quite sure what that purpose was. Then, I found myself back in my bed, and though I didn't remember much, I felt wonderful. It was though the purpose of my life had meaning.

Nissan Dovid Dubov, in his article "The Soul and Afterlife," writes that "the Talmud speaks of 'Heavenly academies' (*Metivta D'Rkia*), where souls sit and learn Torah." It would seem that in my dream I had stumbled into one of these celestial academies.

According to Dubov, the Talmud states:

> "Happy is the man who enters the World to Come with the Talmud in his hand." What one learned in this world is relearned on a much higher level in the next. As is explained in the chapter on Torah learning (ch. 24), there are numerous levels of Torah learning called *Pardes,* and they correspond to the four worlds. The Torah one has learned on the level of *Pshat,* "simple interpretation," one will merit to learn on the level of *Remez* (allusion), *Drush* (homiletics), and *Sod* (secrets). On occasion, souls will be allowed to hear new interpretations in Torah from higher souls. It is said that on the Yartziet of a Tzaddik (righteous person) all other righteous souls come and hear Torah from the Tzaddik.

These levels of learning available to souls in the world to come are amazing.

DEATHBED VISIONS OF DECEASED RELATIVES

I've tried going out in public and sharing accounts like these—of early deathbed visions and experiences and of information about the world to come in the Talmud—to let skeptics and those who are trying to reinvent the wheel know that these experiences have been going on for a very long time. They often look at me and tell me I don't know what I'm talking about. I'll never forget when one guy came up to me after a lecture and tried to tell me the term *deathbed vision* was not what a predeath afterlife encounter was called. He told me I had it all wrong because another author he had read had called it something else.

The term *deathbed vision* was coined by Sir William Barrett (1844–1925). In the early 1920s he wrote *Deathbed Visions,* one of the first definitive modern-era books on this phenomenon. But the thought that afterlife contact is something new—that some modern-day thinker, philosopher, or lecturer came up with this first—always has me running back to Jewish antiquity.

> *And Abraham breathed his last, dying at a good ripe age,*
> *old and contented; and he was gathered to his kin.*
> —GENESIS 25:8

It is said that Abram or Abraham lived 175 years (2150–1975 BCE). Abraham was the first of the Hebrew patriarchs venerated by the three great religions believing in one God—Judaism, Christianity, and Islam. For our purpose it's important to recognize how the departing visions of Abraham are just like many of those documented today. As we will see, as death approaches visions of deceased relatives are not uncommon.

Rabbi Yaakov's message at the beginning of this chapter about the world to come basically says the world we live in is not the only sphere of existence. Sadly, because there isn't an open recognition of a world to come, should we just ignore the rabbi's words, along with our spiritual evolution? Or can we at least, with healthy as opposed to rigid skepticism, look at what might happen when our time to leave the planet ends? After leaving the world of the material, will we enter another world?

At one time, life after death was an unquestionable event. Attention was focused on both humanities and our continued spiritual evolution. This has nothing to do with working for that ticket to heaven. We are encouraged to do what we can for the environment where we currently reside, understanding this is only a small part of the journey. "I am an alien and a resident among you" (Genesis 23:4).

Here is a simple example of the above. When I go to England on business, I'm not going as a resident. As a visitor I could be presenting a workshop. In the process of putting together the presentation, I pay attention to those ideas that would increase my own self-awareness. One might say I spiritually progress. On the flip side this workshop might include information that could help the participants grow and begin their path of self-exploration. Yes, my participation with humanity, my temporary state of existence in this English universe, is to not only help others but also to evolve myself spiritually. My stays across the pond, just like this current life of mine, are not permanent. I'm an alien. I'm just visiting and learning. Once I make that nine-hour trip back from England to Galveston Island in the Gulf of Mexico where I and my family permanently live, I'm a resident—just as I will be once I leave this physical body and return to where I was before this life.

Jewish mysticism and exploration into afterlife encounters can be found in ancient literature like the Talmud (fourth century CE), Torah (1280–1312 BCE), and the Zohar (second century CE). The Jewish mystical writings of the Sefer Ha-Zohar (the Book of Splendor) are said to have first been revealed by God to Moses at Sinai. Then they were passed on down orally as teachings. Finally, they were written down by Rabbi Shimon bar Yochai, a second-century Palestinian rabbi; however, his authorship of the Zohar continues to be debated today. Regardless of who wrote these works, it should be noted that contained within these pages are departing or deathbed visions. These historical encounters are discussed in some detail.

Thus, the Zohar teaches that "at the time of a man's death he is allowed to see his relatives and companions from the other world" (Zohar 1:218a). Similarly, "we have learned that when a man's soul departs from him, all his relatives and companions in the other world join in and show it the place of delight" (Zohar 1:219a).

Then there is the near-death account of Rabbi Shmelke of Sasov from *Tales of the Hasidim* by Martin Buber. Shortly before the death of this famous historic rabbi, he saw standing beside him his deceased father, Rabbi Moshe Leib, and his great teacher, Rabbi Mikhal of Zlotchov.

DESCRIPTIONS OF THE AFTERLIFE: ANCIENT AND MODERN

In the world to come, there is nothing corporeal, and no material substance; there are only souls of the righteous without bodies—like the ministering angels. . . . The righteous attain to a knowledge and realization of truth concerning God to which they had not attained while they were in the murky and lowly body.

—MAIMONIDES, MISHNEH TORAH,
REPENTANCE 8:1

This quote from the Mishneh Torah provides a twelfth-century CE description of the afterlife. Now compare this to the modern-day experience described below.

The following afterlife narrative involves an incredible departing vision. During this time, a woman who has lived for years with the wreckage of an unthinkable loss finally experiences a reunion with loved ones she never thought she'd see again. The story is told by the woman's daughter, Dorothy.

Loss Created by the Holocaust
Followed by a Reunion
Dorothy

My parents were both from Greece, both concentration camp survivors. My father lost all but one brother, a couple of cousins, and one aunt. My mother lost her entire family in Auschwitz. They met after liberation, fell in love, and married. After my oldest brother and I were born in Greece, they immigrated to the United States. Here, we grew up along with two younger brothers and a sister.

Two and a half years ago, my father died following a heart attack and stroke that left his brain destroyed, with no chance of recovery. One night, after being bedridden by illness for three weeks, he sat up in bed, reached his arms into the air, and then lay back dead. As he reached up, my mother had said, "Go to your Mamika, darling"—referring to his mother. Mamika is a Greek term of endearment for "mother."

With my father's passing, my mother's grief was deep. My father was the first person she had loved after losing so many loved ones in the Birkenau and Auschwitz concentration camps. She just wanted to die. It was an impossible situation, and her heartbreak over my father's death was so intense. With heartbreak came stomach pains. After many tests, they opened her up to discover her insides were riddled with cancer. They immediately closed her up. There was nothing to do but send her home to die.

At that time, I was living in New York with a very lucrative career in the entertainment industry. The minute the doctors said it was over, I quit my job, sold my co-op, returned home, and spent the rest of my mother's life with her. My family and I were on death watch. One morning, she kept saying something in Greek. None of us speak Greek, so I called Betty, a friend whose aunt Linda had been my mother's friend; Linda had died in Auschwitz. Betty translated the words as best as she could as a kind of storm, but not a weather storm, more like a happening, a big celebration, and a storm of people. Betty then offered to come over to help take care of the family, cook, and be there if my mother started speaking Greek again. Betty's own parents and sister had passed away, as had her daughter Diane, who had recently died at age twenty-six, and my mother had been a surrogate mother to her.

So, Betty came over and started cooking. Later, my mother started calling her by her Greek name, Bondi. She rushed into my mother's room asking, "What is it, Solica?" My mother was speaking to her in Greek, and as Betty responded to Mother in Greek, she also translated for us what was being said. "Your mother is here cooking," my mother said to her, and Betty replied, "No, I'm here cooking." My mother then said, "Bondi, I know you are here cooking for my children and grandchildren, but your mother and aunt are cooking, too, for the celebration." My mother then added, "Diane is also here." With this, Betty began to sob. Then my mother began greeting other deceased members of her family, telling them where they were going to sit. Her eyes were closed, and her hand moved around the bedspread.

"Henriette will sit here, Mamika here—and where's Bella? Has anyone seen her?" She continued to seat my father and everyone in her family, except for her adored older sister, Bella, who wasn't there. When the youngest brother joined the group, she put her hand up in the air and in a delighted voice said, "Oh, Leoniki, hi!" This continued for nearly an hour, and it's mostly on tape, as I turned on the tape recorder, but it's in Greek!

We were all awed, amazed, and comforted. We were all crying at how beautiful this was. And there were ten of us in the room who witnessed this. In the middle of the night, she started speaking to someone in Spanish. As we are Sephardic Jews, both Spanish and Greek were spoken in my mother's girlhood home. She kept saying Bella.

My older brother, Jerry, and his wife were in the guest room. He speaks Spanish fluently. He asked my mother to whom she was talking, and she said, "Bella." He asked her where she was, and she said, "Bella's house." He then asked her what they were discussing, and she said, "Bella wants me to go for a walk with her." "What are you telling her, Mom?" he asked. She replied, "That I'm not ready to go for a walk yet." She talked a bit more to Bella, and that was all they discussed, going for a walk.

Two days later; my mother passed in the night, as she softly called out to her sister Bella. I feel confident that her adored older sister came to get her to take her to the celebration, as all those on the other side missed her so much. The gift of my mother's visions has had a powerful influence on my life. Although I was raised Jewish, I didn't know a lot about it. So, I decided to go on a spiritual journey to learn more about the mystical side of Judaism and have found a sense of peace. I am not afraid to die, as I know my parents and friends who have gone before me will come back to get me.

My priorities in life are completely different. I spent years in the entertainment industry, and although it was a very good time, I never had the serenity I have now. All the stress that friends have seen on my face is gone. I don't know yet what I want to do with the second act of my life, but I do know it includes public service. I spend all the time I can volunteering for various organizations. I deliver Meals on Wheels to the elderly and homebound twice a week, volunteer in a hospital emergency room three times a week, and help once in a while with other organizations and special events, such as fundraising.

Not long ago, I received an email from Dorothy. She shared with me that her niece and nephew had recently celebrated their bat mitzvah and bar mitzvah. The whole family had come together for this joyous occasion. She also added that the family had strongly sensed the presence of her beloved parents. Death cannot separate the love that bonds a family together.

In this departing vision we see many characteristics that are like those presented previously. Again, we have individuals with Holocaust history who thought they would never see their loved ones again. Instead, they experienced a grand reunion. Second, like my aunt who started speaking Polish as physical death drew near, Greek and even Spanish emerged front and center for this family. The language one grew up with seems to be the tongue spoken as one reunites with old-world relatives in spirit. I had a very good friend who was German. When the Russians moved into what was formerly East Germany, she was placed in a concentration camp at twelve years of age. At the end of her life, I was at her side. As she lay dying, she suddenly started speaking German. When her husband asked me, "What do I do?" I replied, "Talk back to her in German. Ask questions. Let her know you are here." All her life she was a staunch atheist. As she took her last few breaths, she was speaking in German with relatives who had passed on.

We begin to see why those deceased loved ones who greet us aren't necessarily a fantasy. The grocery clerk at our grocery store, our mailman, or that one person we met at a dinner party are not those who reach out to us. No, instead we will be greeted by special departed loved ones. Along with this we might even catch a glimpse of a world to come.

Ancient philosophical, religious commentary and discussion often talk about the dying seeing a gathering of relatives, souls, or angels. Such reunions aren't just found within a few specific religions or ideologies. These reported experiences come from cultures around the globe, and Judaism is no exception.

The Zohar also discusses family visitations from the spirit world. As one prepares to pass, those who have previously physically died fill the room. "At the hour of a man's departure from the world, his father and his relatives gather round him, and he sees them and recognizes them, and likewise all with whom he associated in this world, and they accompany his soul to the place where it is to abide" (Zohar I, 218a).

The Jewish idea of different worlds to come or realms of existence can be found century to century and on down to present date. Like our ancestors, we too can experience afterlife encounters. The following account comes from a very unlikely source. Interestingly, it too reflects those already presented.

Tikvah: Which Means Hope

Tikvah Feinstein, born in Pittsburgh, Pennsylvania, in 1944, has lived an interesting but difficult life. She's a well-known activist, an award-winning fiction and poetry writer, the founder and director of Taproot Writer's Workshop, and the editor and publisher of *Taproot Literature Review*. Feinstein has published several books, including *Music from a Broken Violin: A Memoir* (2011) and *Inanna of Tiamat: A Prehistorical Adventure More True Than Fiction* (1997).

During her early years she was sexually assaulted by a rabbi. This didn't stop her journey. While continuing to explore spirituality, she stayed true to her Jewish roots. In doing so, she discovered that David Horowitz, the man she thought was her uncle, was her biological father.

He wasn't just any Jewish man: Horowitz was a well-known diplomat with the United Nations. According to an article in the *United Israel Bulletin,* Horowitz "functioned as an 'unofficial' Zionist lobbyist and influenced the votes of three critical Central American states in the UN vote for the partition of Palestine on November 29, 1947." Horowitz, an ardent Zionist, founded the United Israel World Union, of which Feinstein is a board member. He assisted in publishing a much-debated translation of scriptures titled *The Bible in the Hands of Its Creators: Biblical Facts as They Are* by Moses Guibbory. In this controversial work Guibbory claimed there was more than just one creator.

In 2001 Feinstein received a letter addressed to her at Taproot Press that contained spores of *Bacillus anthracis,* the bacterium that causes anthrax, an infectious disease. Unfortunately, she opened the envelope, and then found herself in the hospital with respiratory and congestive heart failure. That year a number of letters containing powdered anthrax spores were sent through the U.S. postal system. At that time physicians just called the event a mystery and said her illness could have been caused by a virus. It's possible that this exposure weakened her heart and led to her later heart attack and near-death experience.

In February 2007 Feinstein experienced clinical death. While at a grocery store, she suffered a heart attack and a direct head injury. Her heart was not beating, she was not breathing, and there was no brain function. For all intents and purposes, she was dead. An emergency medical team quickly arrived at the store and gave her CPR. Feinstein was also shocked with paddles multiple times. She revived, and two days later a St. Jude pacemaker was placed in her chest.

Below is her wonderful near-death account.

The Right Grocery Store
Tikvah Feinstein

I awoke on February 5, 2007, feeling like there was danger, like I had to leave my house. When I left the house that morning, I first drove to a grocery store. Then on a whim, I decided to go instead to Foodland. If I had stayed home and the cardiac arrest had happened there, I would not have survived. If I had stayed at the first grocery store and the cardiac arrest had happened there, my chances of surviving would not have been very good. My intuition put me in a place where I could be saved.

Going into the store, I felt my heart palpitate. I was experiencing the beginning of a heart attack. You are supposed to cough, which I did. I then collapsed and struck the back of my head.

I floated above the store. I could hear everything, clear auditory, no distance, saw chaos. I heard my dad, who is deceased, coming. I saw my stepdad, a distinct image. Looking at him I thought—wow! Then there was someone with me, a being who moved ahead. I saw shapes. I thought, "This is where we always are. We are one big organism."

I woke up in the ambulance, heard the ambulance. It was heavy coming back into my body. Life felt constricted here. Changed, I thought about that connection I had experienced, realizing retaliation is not okay. I would not hurt others. Kindness does get misrepresented as weakness.

I am grateful to be among the 5 or so percent who retain their mental resources after clinical death.

Feinstein not only survived but also took away from her experience a knowing that there is no such thing as death. During this time, she saw her deceased biological father and stepfather. Along with this she came back with a powerful message: "Kindness is the greatest of human assets." Yes, she'd had a life-changing encounter with the spirit world.

Hasidic commentary, literature, and documentation are chock-full of afterlife encounters identical to Feinstein's. Very detailed in description, these accounts read as clear as a bell. We are all part of something much greater than ourselves.

Rabbi Schneur Zalman of Liadi, shortly before his death, turned to his grandson and asked, "Do you see anything?" The boy looked at him in astonishment. Then the rebbe said: "All I can see is the divine nothingness which gives life to the world" (from Martin Buber, *Tales of the Hasidim*).

Is religion is a man-made experience or not? Certain paths embracing a particular philosophy and set of rules, even atheistic or agnostic beliefs, put forth a message that says, "Please believe the way we do. You are oh so wrong. There is no room for debate. Free thinking can be a danger because this could remove you from our path, leaving us to question our doctrine and this threatens our way of thinking." Looking at religion, we learn free thinking can at times be very threatening. In doing this we might have more insight into why some members of the Jewish community wish to block out any form of spirituality. Spirituality is an inside job, and this involves some effort. Here we begin to look at all we know about religion and spirituality. After we have done this, it's important to ask ourselves, what out of this pile do we like, just tolerate, or dislike?

THREE

An Angel Named Damus

Heaven is wonderful but getting there is most of the fun.
—The Chofetz Chaim

Unlike Rabbi Yisrael Meir Kagan (1838–1933), commonly known as the Chofetz Chaim, many Jews do not believe in an afterlife and will forcefully try to make their case. Radio host Howard Stern is a perfect example. Like many agnostics and atheists, excessive tragedy can be found in the famous "Shock Jock's" family history.

Stern has Polish Austro-Hungarian ancestry. Both his parents were born in the United States. According to the Howard Stern website, his father, Ben, during a taped interview with Stern, talked about how three of his siblings died as children. Not long after this, Ben's mother was struck by a car and died. Stern's mother, Ray, shared with her young son how her father came close to leaving her and her sister in an orphanage after Ray's own mother died at a young age. "These are the stories I grew up with!" said Stern. These tragedies would naturally create a great sense of anguish, unresolved guilt, and possibly anger. Unaddressed in a healthy manner, the feelings related to these tragedies can then trickle on down the family tree. Such trauma could impact the following generations for decades.

Though Stern has been accused of being a self-hating Jew, I think some of his actions have had more to do with his history. Sadly, the Stern family tree may now need to heal from the feelings passed on down from one generation to the next. Sharing frightening stories and not allowing children to react or have their emotions about this is one more form of the no-talk rule.

Stern's parents began to practice Transcendental Meditation in the early 1970s. They also encouraged him to learn this practice. In an interview with comedian Jerry Seinfeld, Stern discussed TM and credited the technique with helping him quit smoking, achieve his goals in radio, beat an obsessive-compulsive disorder, and cure his mother of depression. Stern has let his radio followers know he's not a fan of Judaism. Leaving Judaism for another path to address concerns such as his is not uncommon.

In November 2000 Stern interviewed me on his show. I called in to discuss my book *One Last Hug before I Go: The Mystery and Meaning of Deathbed Visions* and my interviews of people on their deathbeds. As I was discussing their departing visions, Robin Quivers, a cohost on the show, emotionally stomped on me every time I opened my mouth. I'm a tough cookie, but after a few minutes of conversation, I found myself wondering why on earth I hadn't I thrown in the towel at the beginning of the interview. During the interview, Stern suggested that what people were seeing on their deathbeds were just hallucinations and held firm to his belief that nothing happens when you die. Stern is quoted as saying: "Here's what happens when you die—you sit in a box and get eaten by worms. I guarantee you that when you die, nothing cool happens."

I've heard many Holocaust survivors, including my father-in-law, along with members of following generations express similar views.

At his daughter's bat mitzvah, he jokingly said he hated Jews. Stern also let it be known he detested wearing yarmulkes. Interestingly, in recent years, it appears his harsh beliefs about the traditions he grew up with aren't quite as punitive as they used to be. His eldest daughter, Emily, began to practice Orthodox Judaism around a decade or so ago. It's not uncommon for the children of atheists or agnostics to become religious. Today Howard Stern's daughter is a bit of a Torah scholar. She has also been public about how she doesn't date. In a 2015 *New York Post* story, Emily said her father's excessive sexual talk on his radio show had discouraged her from dating. This is an example of reactions to the feelings or behavior of the previous generation when the sharing of tragic history is not done in a healthy way. Regardless of their differences, Stern had this to say, in the same *Post* article, about his daughter's religious practices: "F--- it if [people] think it's weird or doesn't make sense." I say good for him!

Unaddressed tragedies in previous generations, the feelings of unresolved grief, depression, loneliness, anger, fear, spiritual confusion, shame, and more can move from one generation to the next. If I'd known about Stern's family history before going on his show, I suspect I'd have handled the situation very differently. That said, I do know someone in the audience needed to hear what I had to say. After the show I received tons of email from individuals who had never shared their afterlife encounters with anyone. Who knows, during the radio program maybe Stern picked up a few things to think about.

Speaking of the trickle-down effect on the family tree, let's look at the following account. This woman directly suffered from the Holocaust. Notice how this afterlife event changed her third-generation grandson, who recounts this tale.

I Saw My Grandmother's Soul
Leave Her Body
Salvador Litvak

I know the soul exists. Perhaps that's not a big claim given how often people talk about souls. In addition to the quotes above, Google lists 3.2 billion more. Despite all that attention, however, it remains difficult to know what the soul is, and how it affects our lives.

Jewish mysticism offers answers, as do many other traditions, but hearing someone else's definitions of the soul and its various levels doesn't make my soul real to me—at least not the way my hands and my heart are real. I see my hands typing. I feel my heart beating.

I always wanted my soul to feel viscerally real because I sensed that would prove our Creator did more than fabricate the galaxies. Feeling my soul would mean I have an ongoing connection with G-d.

And now my soul is real to me, thanks to three experiences. The first two happened 17 years ago and redirected the course of my life. The third happened a few days ago, and I don't yet know how it will affect me.

In 1997, my grandmother lay dying in our family home. Her name was Magda, but I called her Ita, short for abuelita—an affectionate term for grandmother in Spanish. She was a Hungarian survivor of the Holocaust, as is my mom, Katalina. Ita carried infant Kati through Theresienstadt, a concentration camp from which only 100 children emerged. Ita helped care for most of them.

My grandfather Imre perished at Dachau. I have a silver cigarette case that Ita gave Imre on their wedding day in 1932. How she loved that man! He was ten years older—the beloved veterinarian of a small farming community that often compensated him with chickens and vegetables for his work.

Ita and Imre tried for years to have children. Their miracle baby arrived in 1944—an impossible time to for a Jew to be born in Europe. Kati never met her father.

Ita never stopped loving Imre. For 53 years she waited to be reunited with him, never even going on a date. She poured her love into her daughter, and then her grandsons—my brother and me.

She sounds saintly and she was, but she was also funny.

"Ita, I think we're gonna get that cable box. We'll have 23 channels!"

"Now I know you're pulling my leg! Who in the world needs 23 channels?!"

She made such a funny face that I had to mirror her expression. My imitation cracked her up, I cracked up in return, and we laughed on and on in a wonderful feedback loop. This happened all the time.

We spoke Spanish because I was born in Chile. Ita (my grandmother) and my mom moved to Chile in 1956, after they finally escaped from the Soviets. In the beginning they liked the Russians for liberating the camps, but those feelings changed in the face of Soviet oppression. We left Chile in 1970, when socialism raised too many red flags for Ita and Kati, survivors of Nazism and Communism.

As a two-time refugee, Ita was always prepared. We had a huge closet in the kitchen and a whole wall full of food in the garage. Should a bit of shelf space become available in either location, Ita would hasten off to the supermarket. She didn't drive, and it was two miles each way. She walked fast.

My family wasn't religious, but Ita was. She prayed alone at night, from her little Hungarian siddur. I never knew what she was saying.

When she lay dying of melanoma at age 88, we all gathered around her. There was a lot of weeping during her final moments, but I stared into her eyes as she took her last breath. And then it happened.

I saw an opening in the air beside her. It was sort of kaleidoscopic around the outside, but mostly blue. Through the opening, I saw Ita rise. She looked old but healthy—the Ita I knew so well.

She didn't see me because she was moving toward someone else. It was my grandfather Imre, whom I recognized from pictures. He was as young and handsome as the last time she'd seen him.

To my surprise, she did not rush forward. In fact, she did not look happy. She seemed embarrassed to be so old, and afraid that he would reject her.

Imre opened his arms. She approached sheepishly. He pulled her close and embraced her. The light surrounding them grew very bright. She became young again, and radiated happiness. They kissed, the light surrounded them, and they were gone.

I saw their souls the way I now see my hands.

When I returned to LA it happened again. I hadn't been to a synagogue in years, but I attended a Shabbat service to honor Ita. During the le-dor va-dor prayer (from generation to generation) I saw two columns of souls towering above me like vast cathedral arches. I knew they were the souls of my ancestors welcoming me back to our tradition. My eyes poured tears—absolute waterworks.

I reconnected with Judaism in that moment, and I've been grateful ever since. I seek out inspiring teachers, music, and community. I've been blessed to find so many.

That's how I know souls exist. I never felt my own soul, however, until a few days ago.

In receiving a glimpse of the world to come, a profound family of origin transformation took place. The sadness of the Holocaust began to lose its impact. Knowing that a departed loved one doesn't just evaporate into nothingness, realizing a spark of life continues once we shed our physical bodies, not only allows us to be more open to our family of origin traumas but also encourages us to heal ourselves.

The next narrative is a personal one. I took a big risk sharing this on the *Howard Stern Show,* but afterward I knew the potential risk for me was worth it.

WHO IS DAMUS?

My father-in-law, a witness to the horrors of the Holocaust, was sick, and the prognosis was not good. Life had been rotating around his illness for many months.

I was way behind on my household chores, including grocery shopping, and knew I had to replenish my cupboards. Every few months, I'd trek to the mainland for what my children call "Momma's weird food." My traveling companion for one such car trip, my three-year-old son, Joshua, was exhausted, hot, hungry, and too tired to even take a nap.

I knew he was dog-tired because he was sitting in the back seat, rubbing his eyes, and crying, "Come back there right now!" Knowing I was in for a battle, I decided to try logic. "Well, honey, if I come to the backseat with you, who will drive the car?"

My young son looked at me with extreme annoyance. "Let Damus drive! He can drive!" Checking my rearview mirror to make sure I didn't have another passenger with me, I asked, "Josh, who is Damus?" With exasperation and a yawn, Josh replied, "Damus is right here, Momma. Now let him drive the car!" No longer in a mood to argue, I said, "Damus can't drive." There! I thought. That should settle this! It didn't. Looking stunned, Josh replied, "How do you know?"

The next day, Josh and I were again on the go when I suddenly remembered Damus. I decided to ask Joshua a few questions about his friend. "Honey, who is Damus?" With a look of frustration, he replied, "Oh, he's just some kid from the sky. A kid with red hair."

A kid from the sky! With red hair? I silently moaned. I decided I needed to know more about this Damus character.

"Sweetie, how long has Damus been around?" I asked, keeping one eye on the rearview mirror and another on the beachfront street.

"Oh, Damus just got here a few days ago," answered my son as he attacked the backseat with his stuffed dinosaur. "Damus just got here?" I asked. "Is he a friend of yours?"

Still growling away, Josh said, "No, Mom! He just got here! He came here for Da!" Da was what the boys called their bigger-than-life grandfather who had found relatives still alive in concentration camps at the end of World War II.

I then pulled the car onto the beach, turned off the engine, faced my son, and asked, "Joshie, is Damus here right now?" His green eyes were already taking in the waves and his only thought was to get out of the car and go play in the sand.

"Momma, can I go play in the water? Let's build a sandcastle!!"

Once again, I asked, "Honey, is Damus here?"

"No, Mom. He isn't here right now. He only comes when he wants to!" He then started to crawl out of his supposedly childproof car seat. Obviously, Damus wasn't as important to him as getting to the shore. After playing in the ocean and running our errands, we were off again. Once in the car, I asked Josh if Damus was back. He looked to the seat beside him, smiled, and said, "Yes." I couldn't see a thing, so I asked, "What does Damus look like, honey?"

Returning his gaze to the seat next to him, Josh answered, "Mom, he looks just like a big kid." With this, he picked up the seashells he had collected and returned to his play.

While Da's condition continued to deteriorate, Damus was with us for the rest of November. Occasionally, Josh would announce that Damus was back, and all of us, myself, my husband, Michael, and my older son, Aaron, would turn to catch a glimpse of this elusive creature. None of us ever saw Damus, and this left Joshua feeling very confused.

On Thanksgiving Day my father-in-law was out of the hospital. After piling him into his fancy wheelchair, he and my mother-in-law joined us for a traditional holiday feast. Everyone had a great time. Da was looking better than he had in weeks, and his wit was back.

The day after Thanksgiving, Da was hit with a huge stroke that completely paralyzed him. Because of this, he was no longer able to eat or talk. The kids were absolutely devastated, especially my older son, Aaron, who worshipped his Da. This major stroke was very difficult for my father-in-law to face. For years he practiced as an eye surgeon. This Frenchman who was used to giving orders was not used to being out of control. To see him lying helpless in a hospital bed was heartbreaking.

December crept into our lives. It was the season of Hanukkah, a favorite occasion of the year for my sons. With potato pancakes, candles, laughter, and more good food, Hanukkah was a time to be with friends and family. Sadly, the season was difficult that year. Da was moving on from this world to whatever the next destination looked like, and we all knew it. The only question was when. Despite Da's condition, we wanted the boys to have their eight nights of lights. Their Da would have wanted this for them, too.

One evening, we were hosting our annual Hanukkah dinner. The house was full of loving friends. Michael and I were bursting into tears every five minutes, while our wonderful friends took turns holding us and providing words of comfort. The stress was incredible and starting to take its toll. Everybody pitched in, so we could make the party happen. After the Hanukkah candles were lit, the latkes devoured, and the wrappings of the presents scattered across the floor, my oldest son asked, "What will happen to Da when he dies?"

Our family had always been very open about death, but still both of my young sons were full of questions. Josh reminded us all that Damus would take Da to the sky, but my oldest boy wasn't buying it. His grief was too big. As a card-carrying member of the afterlife exploration crowd, I could share with my children vivid tales of people who were close to death, yet who returned to life describing visions of heavenly landscapes. Then I decided to tell my boys an experience I'd had with my own mother when she was passing.

As I shared earlier, my beloved mother, Carol, died when I was barely sixteen. She was just thirty-three when diagnosed with breast cancer. Back then, treatment for this disease was hit-and-miss at best. By the time her thirty-eighth birthday rolled around, she was on her deathbed. At five in the morning, moments before her passing, I awoke from a deep sleep and knew intuitively that my mother was dying in the hospital. A chill ran down my spine as I got out of bed, put on my fuzzy pink bathrobe, and went downstairs to sit by the phone. Alone in the early dawn, I could feel the sadness penetrating every cell of my being. As the sun came up over the backyard orchard of fruit trees, the tears began to slowly slide down my cheeks. My beautiful, vivacious mother had moved on, and I knew it. About fifteen minutes later, the phone rang. Picking up the receiver I said, "Yes, I already know."

At this same time, two very good family friends were also getting out of their beds and slipping into bathrobes. They too had suddenly awakened at 5:00 a.m., miles away from the hospital in separate locations. When their eyes opened, they also knew my mother was departing this world and making her way to the next.

Not far from where I lived, my great aunt and cousin were talking on the phone. Both lived way up in the California mountains, miles from the hospital caring for my mother. My great aunt had awoken from a dream about my mother leaving. Talking with her daughter, my cousin, she said, "Carol has left us." In response my cousin Virginia said, "Mom, I already know."

At the same moment, all five of us had known and felt my mother leaving for the next journey. Before slipping through the veil and onward to a world to come, a part of her had reached out to touch us. My mother gave each of us one final good-bye hug before she left.

When I shared this encounter with my family, their expressions turned to wonder. Then I was confronted with a multitude of questions about life after death. My experience with my mother's physical passing had proved to me that some thing, or some part of us survives after the physical body dies. I explained to both family and friends that a departing vision is a precious otherworldly encounter. I added that we or those who are dying can experience a departing vision moments, minutes, days, weeks, or months before the actual physical death. This event can happen for the one who is passing or for the survivors.

After talking with my boys, my husband pulled me aside and asked, "Do you think Josh is having departing visions?" Startled by Michael's eye-opening revelation I replied, "You just might be on to something. Damus didn't show up until Da was really sick, and Josh said Damus was here to take Da away."

That evening, Michael decided he needed some time alone with his father. I had just put the kids to bed when Michael let me know he was going to spend the night with Da at the hospital. I packed up some freshly baked cookies and sent them and my husband to see Da. The next morning, my tired husband returned home looking ragged around the edges. Despite appearances, he seemed at peace.

I could tell Michael was eager to talk. With a look of amazement, he said, "You won't believe what happened last night."

Totally confused, I asked, "Has Da moved on?"

"Oh no. It's nothing like that," he answered. "Last night, at about four in the morning, I had the weirdest experience." As a child of family impacted by the Holocaust, I knew my husband was not one to share openly, so I knew I needed to remain quiet and listen. "It was about four in the morning," he repeated, "and I was sleeping in the big chair next to Da's bed. I awoke to see this swirl of pastel color rising from Da's chest. He looked so peaceful as this light swirl of . . . I don't know what . . . continued to rise." Then he asked, "Da is going to die soon, isn't he?" Michael had tears rolling down his cheeks.

"Yes," I replied.

Later that day, I talked to my cousin Yvonne. She also had had a strange experience during her mother's passing. "The paramedics had arrived, but Dad and I knew they were too late. I sat there with my mother as she passed and watched this gray wisp of vapor leave her body. As it disappeared, I knew Mother was gone."

After sharing Michael's experience with her, she said, "Yeah, sounds like Da is getting ready to leave us."

Da Picks a Time to Leave Us

It was Friday the thirteenth. We took a break from the hospital and rounded up the boys for a family night service at our temple. At that time, we belonged to a great Jewish community where the rabbi was called Jimmy and children could run wild through the temple halls when they needed to burn off energy. Once a month, many of the families in the congregation would bring food for a big meal after services.

One Shabbos evening, after we had eaten, I pulled Jimmy aside and asked him if he had ever heard the word *damus*. This was all I shared with him. He suddenly pulled his pen out of his shirt pocket and started writing in Aramaic and then Hebrew. After pondering his writings, he looked up and said, "Damus, Damas, or Duhma, depending on the spelling, translates to 'messenger of death.' According to our tradition, the messenger of death or angel of death is a being who helps those who are dying. Dumah is the name of the angel who has charge of souls in the nether world. Where did you hear this term? It isn't that common."

I was speechless! I didn't know what to say. My young son had been having departing visions. Suddenly, I started to cry. Rabbi Jimmy found my response somewhat alarming and asked "What's up?" While blowing my nose I shared with him about our strange visitor. His only response was "wow!"

Earlier that day, we had moved Da from the hospital back to his room at a local residential care facility, a block from our home. Both Michael and I believed he knew his physical death was near. We had always known he was adamant about not dying in a hospital, so once back in his own room, with his familiar blankets, comforter, and pillows, Da seemed to relax. Michael had put a map of the world on the wall next to his bed. When I asked him why he had done this, with tears in his eyes he said, "I thought after Da leaves his body, he could use the map to help him visit all the people and places he so loved. He just loves to travel and has never gone anywhere without at least a dozen maps."

That evening, Michael had also opened Da's window. When I asked him about this, he said, "Something told me to do it. I know this sounds strange, but it was like a nagging thought. It drove me nuts, so I finally gave in and pushed the window wide open." Then knowingly he added, "I bet when Da leaves his spirit will go through that window."

After my visit with Rabbi Jimmy, I had planned on making the nightly trip to Da's bedside and had even hired a babysitter for the evening. Despite my well-thought-out plan, I was beat. Feeling absolutely drained, I decided to put off my visit and take some much-needed quiet time for my own soul. Stretching out on the couch, I wrapped myself in my grandmother's bright blue afghan. One of my tabby cats had just jumped up on the couch and was making himself a bed on my chest when the phone rang. It was Michael.

"He died in my arms, Carla. He waited until the ten o'clock news was over and then he left. Just so like him." With Da's room being just a stone's throw away from our house, I quickly replied, "I love you, and I'll be there in five minutes."

My father-in-law had always been a control freak with a dark sense of humor, and his death experience was totally and completely his. As I moved the cat and stood up, I just had to chuckle. He had waited for Hanukkah to pass because he knew how important the holiday was for his grandsons. Just to get at us all, he had chosen Friday the thirteenth to make his exit. Being a lover of the evening news, he had waited until the ten o'clock broadcast was over before taking flight. Such a trickster, I mused, as I folded the afghan, preparing to join Michael.

Later that evening, after the family had invaded Da's room and our friendly mortician, David, had taken his body away, I returned to my house full of sleeping children and animals. Knowing I needed to tell my oldest son, Aaron, his grandfather had finally died, I composed myself. As I crept into his room, I tripped over a football and then a tennis racket. "Mom? Is that you?" As Aaron rubbed the sleep from his eyes he asked, "What is it? Is it Da?"

Embracing him close to me, I smoothed his tousled hair and said, "Yes, honey. Da left."

As the tears began to spill, my son held me tightly. Aaron sobbed his heart out for a good thirty minutes. After he cried all he could, I told him, "I love you." Then we sat in silence on his bed until he fell asleep.

The next morning, my three-year-old woke me up at the crack of dawn. As he pried my eyes open with his little chubby fingers, I thought to myself, "Oh, I still need to tell Josh about Da." Half awake, I pulled myself out from under the warmth of my favorite afghan and said, "Sweetie, Da died last night, and he went to be with his mom and dad." He climbed onto my bed and snuggled close to me asking, "Did it hurt Da to die?"

I replied, "No, for him it was like walking out one door and into a new room, into a special place." Then the tears came. After a bit he asked, "Will I ever get to see him again?" I replied, "Yes, you will get to walk through that same door one day." "Will it be scary?" he asked. Hugging him tighter I said, "No."

Then Aaron told us he'd had a dream about Da. In this dream his grandfather had come to him to tell him he was okay and that he loved him. He said it was like no dream he had ever had. It was as if his Da was alive and right there. Instead of being in a wheelchair or hospital bed, he was standing. Aaron experienced an after-death contact, where visitations or communications with deceased loved ones in spirit take place. The message typically is, "I'm fine, all is well." This after-death contact gave us comfort.

All of us grieved Da's passing in our own way. We cried and talked about our feelings as they came up. Both Josh and Aaron had lots of questions about death, and we discussed them, time and time again, with honesty and care. Each of us participated in the funeral. When it was time to lay Da's headstone on his grave, we took matters into our own hands, literally.

With Aaron rallying the troops, we laid the stone ourselves as a family. The dirt on the grave was dug, cement was mixed, and then Michael, Aaron, Josh, and I set the two-hundred-pound stone into the ground. Other physical remains of family had been laid in the family plot of the cemetery of this conservative shul or synagogue. Overlooking the bayou and covered with large oaks, we then sat down next to Da's grave. As we did so, all of us had an overwhelming sensation that Da was watching, laughing about being in a conservative cemetery, and wondering what on earth had possessed us to do what we were doing.

After cleaning the dirt off the stone and ourselves, we sat back and drank a few cold sodas. Stories were then told, tales about our Da who had gone to the sky with Damus. After this, we gratefully slid into our air-conditioned car, recognizing we had done what Da would have wanted. The angel Damus never visited again.

> *Then shall the dust return to the earth as it was: and the spirit shall return unto God who gave it.*
>
> —ECCLESIASTES 12:7

If we were to look at the incredible 1512 CE fresco painting found in the Vatican on the ceiling of the Sistine Chapel titled *The Creation of Adam,* we would see how Michelangelo has presented a vision of God passing life onto Adam. Many Jews are not aware that within ancient literature there is a great deal of discussion about the passing on of the spark of life, the god spark or light from a higher creative consciousness. This active universal awareness or spirit supposedly resides within each of us. The soul is often described as breath or light. It is this light, energy, or vibration that moves on. Though Da was an agnostic, borderline atheist, his sacred essence returned to where he had come from.

I like to visualize my soul or spirit as a shard of brilliant, spiritually creative, conscious light infused temporarily within my physical being. Does this take away from my own unique individuality? I don't think so. When a vase breaks into pieces, each portion is unique. No two broken pieces are alike. Though my shard, light, higher consciousness, or breath of life may come from the same source, my fragment is still unique.

This shard of intelligence comes from some higher source or universal energy, a life force within us that does not vanish when we physically die. Albert Einstein (1879–1955) stated years ago (around 1904) that "energy cannot be created or destroyed; it can only be changed from one form to another." All living creatures and minerals are made up of energy at different vibrations. The word *god* is difficult for many of us, so I appreciate concepts like consciousness, universal power, higher power, her, him, it, creator, undefinable, supreme being, a spirit of the universe, or creative intelligence. My favorite term for this universal power is *Ein Sof,* a Hebrew word that means "infinity, unending, no ending," "the infinite" (*ad le-ein sof*), "infinite light," "no definable form, boundless, no static," or no "god in a box." The Jewish concept of Ein Sof says that there is no ending, only infinity.

A God of Our Choice

With modern Judaism there isn't a requirement to be so inflexible about concepts of God. In other words, everyone can pretty much define the god of his or her choice. I share this because many Jews have experienced religious or cultural rigidity in their youth. Eventually, the Judaic door is nailed shut on the whole matter. Then in adulthood, if we do encounter some sort of near-death experience or afterlife encounter, we make sure this door is locked even more securely, thinking, "I can't talk about this. People will just think it's woo-woo stuff!"

As my Russian grandmother would say, "That's just superstitious nonsense." Because she wanted me to live the American dream, she didn't want me saddled with some of the old-world experiences she associated with relatives perishing in gulags. In her mind God had let her down, and she was going to protect me from such emotional disappointment. My husband's father was kicked out of France for being a communist and became a diehard agnostic and at times atheist. In seeing what happened to so many of his family in Europe, he could never reconcile how a loving God could do such a thing, take so much from him.

At this same time, as a child my husband, Michael Brandon, grew up conservatively and was going to Hebrew class four times a week. His mother's grandfather had been a rabbi in Poland, so in her mind such a religious education was a must. Because of this Michael was receiving two mixed messages from his parents and community: there is no God, but you had better follow the principles of this religion or else. A lot of us grew up with such confusion. I believe this is just one of several reasons why the Jewish community has had a hard time embracing their own afterlife encounters.

So far, we've learned we don't have to believe in the god of our ancestors unless we choose to. We also begin to see that Jews like others do experience afterlife contact events. The third thing we must recognize is afterlife events can be found in ancient writings. If we were to compare modern-day accounts with some of these historical encounters, we would see they are almost identical. With this, we might begin exploring the light within, universal creativity, higher source, or Ein Sof. And no, we don't necessarily need to be a Torah scholar to make sense of all of this. If you have a god of your understanding or are confused about any concept of a higher universal intelligence, that's fine. Beginning to acknowledge there are many modern-day afterlife accounts that echo back to historical experiences is one of the insights we are looking for.

> *What separates me from most so-called atheists is a feeling of utter humility toward the unattainable secrets of the harmony of the cosmos.*
>
> —ALBERT EINSTEIN

FOUR

Experiencing Auschwitz with Nuinui

Memory for most is a kind of afterlife: for my mother, it is another form of life.

—FERN SCHUMER CHAPMAN,
MOTHERLAND: BEYOND THE HOLOCAUST

Naomi Warren, my husband's Polish aunt—or Nuinui as we all liked to call her—was a Holocaust survivor who weathered several gruesome death camps. First there was Auschwitz. When Naomi was eighty-three years old, fourteen family members escorted her back to Auschwitz. As we walked through the haunting silence of the death camp, it was here that she finally told the story of how she and other relatives were harshly pushed into crowded cattle cars for a trip to death. The journey was grueling. There were no sanitary conditions, and many prisoners were forced to stand upward during the entire journey. Food was scarce, and the temperatures could reach freezing.

Many perished in those cattle cars, but Naomi, her husband, Alexander, her mother, Chassia, and others survived. After reaching Auschwitz, the Nazis brutally pushed everyone out of the cars and with guns pointed forced terrified men, women, and children into lines. Chassia, being a quick study, suddenly saw where each line led. Both she and her daughter were headed for the gas chambers.

Love and a powerful mothering instinct took over. Chassia quickly pushed her beloved daughter Naomi into the line for the workforce. Sadly, harsh vengeance, including death by deadly gas, guaranteed mother and daughter would never see one another again. For Naomi life at Auschwitz was unimaginable. Starvation, rape, murder, violent abuse, and other life-threatening acts of degradation were just part of daily life at this Nazi death camp.

After surviving the trauma of Auschwitz, Naomi was then sent to Ravensbrück, a notorious women's concentration camp in northern Germany. The infamous Nazi Heinrich Himmler was behind the construction of the deadly housing facility. To fool the Americans, concentration camps were built in northern Germany. Initially, this appeared to be the ideal prison setup. In reality, this would prove to be far from the truth. SS guards were conducting unthinkable medical experiments and sterilizations on women. And this was only the tip of the iceberg for Naomi; worse was to come.

She was next sent to Bergen-Belsen concentration camp, also located in northern Germany. Bergen-Belsen was used by the Nazis as a death camp for those coming from other prisons. Dysentery, tuberculosis, and many other deadly diseases riddled the camp. When my aunt was liberated from Bergen-Belsen on April 15, 1945, she thought this was the beginning of a new carefree life. But though she became an extremely successful business owner, her past followed her.

Alive and safe, Naomi suffered many physical, emotional, and spiritual losses. The images of terror could not be easily erased. Even the removal of an abusively engraved tattoo would not allow normalcy to return. The Nazis had murdered her dear mother, beloved husband, cousins, in-laws, and other loved ones. There was now delicious food on her plate, pretty clothes to wear, and, at the end of the day, soft sheets to snuggle into, but fear remained her constant companion. I watched her work through sorrow and grief, one day at a time.

Because of family losses in Russia under Stalin, I'd become a victim of violence myself. Naomi's healing paved a path for me. She shared words of wisdom with me: "If I can't have 'true' compassion for myself, I will never have 'true' compassion for others." This resonated to the core of my soul. When I'd find myself upset about a health concern, family loss, or some other difficulty, my aunt would also say, "During the Holocaust we had to live! We had to have a positive attitude. Bad things will happen to you, so you do what you can do, what you need to do."

Naomi began to recover by talking about how she treasured her friends in the camps. Even though emaciated and exhausted, these women would get themselves up from the wooden planks on which they had huddled all night. After tightening rags around their skeletal bodies, together they would then go deep into the frigid snowy forests as slave workers. Though death was always near, friendship and devotion kept Naomi alive.

Toward the end of Naomi's life, I was lucky enough to spend a lot of time with her. Along with my husband and sons, we'd travel the forty-five minutes to her place. While eating thick, greasy latkes with sour cream, we would laugh; and then she would begin to recall the bad times and friendships in the camps.

Though her health was deteriorating, we and the rest of the family continued to listen to our aunt's reminiscing of the past. We also chattered and caught up on each other's lives. My aunt was always listening to us. Naomi would even lift a pillow from underneath her head to better hear with both ears. The desire to catch a bit of gossip never leaves us, no matter how old we are. I remember my 105-year-old Russian aunt doing the same thing. Like Naomi, she too remained interested in what was going on with the people she loved until her dying day.

During our last visit I could tell Naomi was having departing visions, visitations from loved ones who had already passed on. Like her sister, my mother-in-law, Lisa, she was having conversations with her mother, Chassia. Along with these animated exchanges, she was also communicating with her father, Samuel. When we heard this, we felt an incredible sense of relief. I knew the visitations would provide a gentle passing for my aunt.

Naomi was talking in Polish to her mother and father. I remembered the many different individuals I'd been with who had returned to their mother tongue before moving to the next realm. Going back to the language of origin, interacting with those in some form of afterlife existence, is more common than not.

The last day I saw my aunt I knew her time had come. Before Rosh Hashanah she would leave her physical body and join in spirit with all those she loved.

NAOMI'S FINAL EXIT

Even into her nineties, my aunt was still a beauty. Be it traveling across the United States or internationally, Naomi knew how to make an entrance. Dressed elegantly she would float into a crowded room. Her laugh was infectious and her intellect obvious. Naomi's exits were a little bit different. She was always one of the remaining people to leave a room. Giving that last hug, final handshake, or kiss on the cheek, one knew she was truly interested in what had just been shared. Her transition from this life to the next was no different. At the end she was still trying to reassure those at her bedside by letting them know they were special in her life and that she would be just fine.

She knew her precious family—including me, my husband (her nephew), and our two sons—were present and sitting on her bed. At the same time, she already had one foot in the world to come. Her encounter with her dear ones in an afterlife mirrored those accounts I'd previously witnessed or experienced. Along with this they echoed those I'd read in the scrolls. Naomi's reunion with her mother, Chassia, who perished in Auschwitz, brought tears to our eyes. Mother and daughter were finally together again.

The Zohar—written during a different era in time and a commentary on the mystical aspects of the Torah and other spiritual writings—describes similar experiences. In this literature Rabbi Shimon asks Rabbi Yitzchak says: "Have you seen your father's image today, or have you not? For we have learned that when a man departs from the world, his father and relatives are there with him, and he sees and recognizes them. And all those whom he will dwell in the other world in the same chamber, all gather to be with him, and accompany his soul to its dwelling place" (Zohar, VaYechi 217a).

Is there a bridge between this world and the next or is this just wishful thinking or imagination? Are we tapping into old-world superstition to bind our fear of physical death? Or are the afterlife encounters of ancestors from ancient times validating our own afterlife experiences? Let's look at the following modern-day account.

PROOF OF THE AFTERLIFE

If you're questioning the authenticity of these accounts, know you aren't alone, especially if you're a scientifically minded individual. Feeling skeptical or just having doubts is not always a bad thing.

A friend of mine, Jeffrey Long, M.D., specializes in radiation oncology. He's also a bestselling author and near-death experience researcher who founded the Near-Death Experience Research Foundation in 1998. Long began his investigations by looking at just how real these events were. In asking those who had encountered near-death experiences (over four thousand analyzed cases), he discovered consistent similarities from person to person, regardless of culture, religious philosophy, or ethnic background. He has documented his research in his book *Evidence of the Afterlife,* coauthored with Paul Perry. After much calculation Long determined that once we slip out of our physical bodies, something takes place for each one of us.

As I mentioned earlier, every day someone asks me: "What happens once we die?" "Where do we go after living this physical life?" "Is this really all there is?" For most of us, not having some sort of answer to these questions can produce life problems. We may find ourselves walking around with fears and phobias about dying, death, anxiety, loss of control, depression, or confusion about why we are living life at all! Unfortunately, most of us are unaware of Long's findings, my examinations, or of the numerous investigators around the globe. The following statement from Long gives us a clue about the amount of information from researchers, investigators, and experiencers available: "There is currently more scientific evidence to the reality of near-death experience (NDE) than there is for how to effectively treat certain forms of cancer." Despite the evidence provided by psychologists, therapists, neuropsychologists, medical nurses, physicians, educators, authors, and NDE experiencers, the societal belief continues to insist that if you can't see it with the naked eye then it doesn't exist.

Peter Fenwick, M.D., another acquaintance of mine, is a neuropsychiatrist and world-famous NDE researcher living in the United Kingdom. Aside from being a fellow at the Royal College of Medicine, Dr. Fenwick has published several books on death and dying. Over the years, he has been involved in a great deal of research on this topic, including work with hospice in the south of England and nursing homes in Holland.

In May 2012 Michael Tymn—who is the editor of the *Journal for Spiritual Consciousness Studies* and *The Searchlight,* both quarterly publications of the Academy of Spirituality and Paranormal Studies—interviewed Fenwick for his White Crow Books blog. During the interview, Fenwick noted that "thirty percent of NDEs reported during a cardiac arrest have an out-of-body experience in which the experiencer reported leaving his body and witnessing the cardiac arrest resuscitation procedure." He said he'd made some very compelling observations about how we view dying and death. He added this could account for why there is so much skepticism about near-death encounters, departing visions, after-death contact, and consciousness.

> Mainstream science has shown little interest in the mental states of the dying, and so many of these phenomena are poorly recorded and studied. The features of the experiences of the dying are not taught in medical schools so doctors know little about them. Consequently, nurses and care workers are reluctant to talk about what they see and experience as these things are not within their culture and not accepted.

Based on my own clinical experiences it appears modern societal institutions don't seem too interested in these matters, leaving us, the public, in the dark ages when it comes to death, dying, and an afterlife. So-called intellectuals within our culture appear to be invested in ignoring the wealth of information available on afterlife contact. This would be an example of the no-talk rule.

Here is an incredibly simplistic example of what I believe is going on. Living just blocks from the sea, I know if I swim away from the beach there is a sandbar. Paddling along with my feet I can't reach it, but I know it's there. I'm also aware there are a variety of sea creatures swimming and living all around me. Do I always see them? The answer is no. So, how am I conscious of their presence? Fishermen are my resource, and when many of them tell me the same thing, I tend to believe them.

If I've stepped on a stingray and you haven't, how will you respond to my experience? Will you believe me? It depends on where you live, your experience, what you've read, and possibly who you've talked to. This is just human nature.

Herein lies the problem. A physically dying person who is having departing visions may report this to those at the bedside. They might say their deceased mother, father, sibling, best friend, past love, or grandparents have come to speak with them on a trip to the afterlife. Because physicians are not visually seeing the same thing as their dying patients, they will often give these individuals antipsychotic, antianxiety, or other psychotropic medication. That's like a doctor overdrugging me for a fear of stingrays based on my personal experience with the fish, even though they themselves don't know what a stingray is.

Why We Need to Keep an Open Mind

Most of my experiences on the earth plane appear to be based on so-called solid encounters. My own childhood belief was that if I couldn't see it I doubted its existence. As we get older, we begin to discover there are many things we can't see with the naked eye. For example, consider the scientific facts, which most of us accept, that the hydrogen atom is about 99 percent empty space and that hydrogen makes up around 90 percent of all other atoms. That's lots of empty space! We accept that the matter of the world is mostly empty space, even though our senses tell us otherwise.

Have I triggered everyone's brain cells to begin synapsing with afterlife thoughts? Has the closed door opened a crack? If you weren't relating to these words before, how about now? No matter what your beliefs, come along and continue to explore the possibility that Jewish afterlife encounters might be real. While on this venture, we may even become more aware of our own history and how this has impacted our acceptance of an afterlife.

FIVE

Where Was God?

*The spirit of man is the candle of the Lord, searching all
the inward parts of the belly.*

—Proverbs 20:27

Holocaust survivor Elie Wiesel, a prolific author, activist, and Nobel Prize winner for Peace, had to examine what he thought of God. While in the camps he waited for the god of his youth to step in and save the Jewish people. When this didn't happen, he blamed this god for the horrific torture and degradation he had experienced and witnessed. Wiesel lost his parents, sisters, uncles, grandparents, and cousins to the death camps. Seeing a crematorium pit, he noted, in his book *Night,* that "for the first time I felt revolt rise up in me. Why should I bless his name?"

Like so many survivors, anger tormented Wiesel, and he lost his faith. Wiesel eventually realized this cruel childhood god wasn't for him. After that enlightenment, he knew God hadn't caused such savagery. God didn't tell the Nazis to murder the Jews. Such pointless losses were not God's will. The will of man's evil intentions had birthed the Holocaust.

FROM HELL TO A CAUSE

"'How do I find God?' you ask. I do not know how, but I do know where-in my fellow man."

With this profound realization Wiesel set upon a journey to reevaluate his relationship with God.

In 1986, while he was being awarded the Nobel Prize for Peace, Wiesel had an after-death contact with his father, Shlomo Wiesel: he saw his father sitting in the hall. The elder Wiesel had perished in the Buchenwald death camp shortly before liberation. While in the hospital undergoing emergency open-heart surgery in 2011, he had another after-death contact with his father. During this same time, Elie Wiesel also had visions of his mother and younger sister. After-death communications come in all forms, but such encounters always involve some type of contact with the deceased.

Oprah Winfrey asked Wiesel, in a 2012 interview on the TV series *Super Soul Sunday:* "What do you think happens when we die?" He replied: "I—we—become a child . . . childhood, for me, is a theme in all my work. We become a child." When Winfrey asked about his vision of family members while he lay in the hospital bed, Wiesel said: "It was almost reassuring. I would not be alone. They are there with me. And that is the danger usually, I think, in being so sick. That's the danger. That you feel it's so good being with the dead, why not join them? It will be a liberation."

When we have an after-death contact with deceased loved ones, this tends to relieve any fear of death. Such events help us to recognize we will not be alone because there is some sort of existence after physical death. There will be somebody there to greet us when it's our time to cross over to the next world. All will be well, and we will continue to spiritually evolve. Most importantly, we recognize what we see in the physical isn't all there is.

FAMILY REUNION

Let's look at the price paid to walk away from spirituality. Samuel and Chassia, the parents of my mother-in-law, Lisa Brandon, were very good to their children. Lisa's grandfather was a learned rabbi, while her father, Samuel, was a successful banker. There were three children, one son and two daughters, Naomi and Lisa. Chassia was the best of cooks, preparing rich noodle kugel, challah, roasted meats, latkes, and fruit compotes. Lisa always said she had a very happy childhood and even admitted she was a bit spoiled.

Lisa attended the Conservatory of Music in Wilno, Poland, and completed her education at the University of Warsaw. After leaving Poland, she earned a master's degree in Paris at the Sorbonne and then a doctorate at Laval University in Quebec, Canada. Despite the trauma and losses of World War II, she was a very accomplished woman, becoming one of the foremost authorities in the French Cajun folklore of Louisiana. People were often unaware of her brilliance. Her couture style, always wearing fashionable heels and a strand of pearls, obscured that here was a feminist and a scientifically minded professor who was also the chair of a major university French department. Lisa believed an evening devoted to arguing politics was a good time. But discussions about the afterlife or religion were a waste of brain cells. And sadly, the Holocaust was also off limits.

Moving forward almost eight decades, the year is 2002. It was a dark and gloomy day on the blustery Gulf Coast. Regardless of the island winds, Lisa's room was cramped and hot. She'd stopped eating and wasn't taking in any liquids. Once this happened, she began calling out to relatives who were physically deceased. These departing visions were profound.

A few hospice workers are familiar with this phenomenon. Sadly, the one caretaker sitting next to Lisa's bedside didn't have a clue. The poor thing began to emotionally unravel as Lisa started having animated discussions with invisible visitors in the room. Immediately, medications for hallucinations were strongly suggested by nurses, and the doctor was called. Many medical professionals don't realize departing visions are common, comforting events, which are more potent than any pill.

Just hours before her passing, Lisa started talking to several specific deceased relatives. While calling them out by name, a few of the living looked confused and even visibly upset. Though I'd been investigating the departing-vision phenomenon for decades, I never dreamed this would be part of my skeptical mother-in-law's "exit script"!

When my first book on the spiritual experiences of the dying was published, she didn't rush to read it. Instead, Lisa let me know she had no time for what she called "superstitious nonsense." One could confidently say she was incredibly cynical about all things spiritual and for good reasons.

In her early twenties, she lost her beloved mother to the Nazi death camp Auschwitz. After such harsh sorrow, her questions then became: "Why did I survive?" "How could six million have been murdered? What kind of god would let this happen?" Knowing this tragic history, Michael and I often spoke of how the Holocaust had been so destructive for her and the entire family.

My father-in-law didn't believe in anything spiritual. As an atheist, he'd attended communist gatherings in France. He refused to set foot in a synagogue in the states. My mother-in-law was also not very religious. When I began working on my second book on the departing visions of the dying, I asked her if she would like to read part of the manuscript. She replied, "I can't read this because I'm not spiritual enough." This broke my heart.

When Lisa became sick, Michael and I would talk about how incredible it would be if she had a departing vision of reuniting with her mother, Chassia. After such discussions, we'd then look at each other and shake our heads no. Both of us were convinced she would go out kicking and screaming. Thankfully, we were wrong. Sitting at Lisa's bedside, watching her frail body give way, I soon learned even skeptical university professors can be surprised.

On the morning of her passing, Lisa became very irritated. She didn't understand her initial departing visions. Her sister Naomi, a Holocaust survivor of three camps, was with us. We watched as the two sisters went into deep conversation about the "visions" or scenarios she was seeing. In Polish Lisa said, "These plays are annoying! Crazy!" My husband's aunt Naomi then turned to my husband and me and asked, "What on earth is she talking about?"

We told Naomi and the rest of the family: "This is normal and it's a good thing. Don't worry." We then shared with them information about departing visions. "The physically dying will revert to the language of their youth, and for Lisa it's Polish." To Naomi I said, "She's being visited by deceased relatives or friends, and we need for you to keep translating for us so that we can know who she's communicating with." Lisa continued to talk to people we couldn't see. This not only eased my aunt Naomi's concern but also soothed her grief.

With the help of Naomi translating, we quickly learned Lisa was having a passionate conversation with my deceased father-in-law, also known to his grandchildren as Da. As she talked back and forth between us and Da, we noticed she was using the word *malpa*. Malpa means "monkey" in Polish, and this was her special nickname for her husband. Though his visit seemed to be reducing her fear of dying, she was still letting him know she wasn't ready to go. Michael and I knew she was stubborn but wondered what was really behind her reluctance to move on.

We continued to watch Lisa call out to Da by his Polish nickname Malpa. Her conversations with him were now very lively, and the more she talked, the more relaxed she became. She even seemed less anxious about leaving us and joining Da in the afterlife. With my father-in-law's visitation, the first step in healing old wounds had been taken. Any remaining fear of death was quickly evaporating. At this point, all Michael and I could do was grin.

As my in-law's reunion went on, the hospice worker at her bedside was growing even more controlling, insisting on strong drugs for "Lisa's significant hallucinations." I could tell underneath her pushy veneer she was downright frightened by what she was seeing.

Lisa was not in pain, and she didn't need potent narcotics. Looking at her chatting away, we knew she was just fine. Sadly, the hospice worker wanted Lisa sedated because she was uncomfortable with the departing visions. The family then voted "no more medications." Regardless, the hospice worker still tried to make us feel guilty. I finally took the poor, now-sobbing woman by the arm, escorted her out of the room, and said, "It's really okay. We can take it from here."

After a short tea break, I returned to Lisa's room and noticed her mood had changed dramatically. She was no longer talking to Da. Now speaking to someone else, her eyes were beginning to well up with tears. Suddenly, Lisa cried out to her mother, Chassia, who had been gassed to death in Auschwitz during the Holocaust. Listening quietly, we realized she was finally confronting an unfathomable grief, one she had carried into her eighties.

Lisa's mother, brother, sister, brother-in-law, cousins, and friends did not know what horrors awaited them when the cattle cars finally stopped in Auschwitz. Once the thick ice covering the inside of the door of the train was broken, the starving found themselves brutally pushed into a scene of chaos. Nazis with guns and snarling attack dogs immediately began to divide families up. Younger people were separated from older family members, as were husbands from wives, and children from parents. Everyone was suffering from malnutrition. Unfortunately, starvation in Auschwitz would only worsen for all. But for Lisa and her family, love was the glue that helped many of them survive.

Back in the states, Lisa didn't know anything about her family. Living with not knowing who was alive or dead for so many months had a lifelong, devastating effect on her. She worried the bonds of love were no more. Survivor's guilt and shame would haunt her for decades. Unresolved grief over the violent death of her mother, Chassia, and other family members would be a persistent wound.

That said, never say never.

Tears were running down our cheeks as Lisa sat up in her bed and called out to her mother, Chassia. This lifelong loss, which had almost destroyed her and been at the core of so much anguish, was finally dissolving before our very eyes. Mother and daughter had found each other. Michael and I were able to witness this. It truly was a grand reunion. Lifelong suffering, which had created such rage and death phobia, was suddenly no more. Now she was almost ready to go.

Lisa was extremely lucid for the rest of the day. When Michael, my boys, or I would speak to her, she would turn and happily chatter back. She knew when we were in the room and constantly told us she loved us. She also hugged her nephews and niece, along with our rabbi, Jimmy Kessler. Being eighty-eight years old and having healed from a lifetime of emotional distress, she finally realized it was time for her to move on. The visitations from her husband, Malpa, and her mother, Chassia, helped her finally begin to let go. Death was nothing to fear.

Another woman shared with me a modern-day encounter like Lisa's. The sting of death was softened with a communication from her deceased husband. Compare this after-death contact to the above accounts. Look for the consistencies.

Three Dogs Barking
Myrna Lou Goldbaum

On December 5, 1980, my forty-two-year-old husband passed away in the hospital from a massive heart attack. I was forty years old at the time, and we had been married twenty years.

I rushed to his room in the hospital but was too late to say good-bye. That night back at home, as I lay in bed with my three dogs, two yellow labs and a mutt, I was awakened by their constant barking. I looked up at the doorway of my room, and there standing in the bedroom hallway was my deceased husband, surrounded by what looked like sparklers from the Fourth of July. As he approached my bed, the dogs ceased barking and wagged their tails, happy to see him.

He floated to my side of the bed and touched my cheek in the way he always had before, which was with the back of his hand going from under my eye to my chin. I knew it was him by that touch and was not afraid. We said good-bye with our eyes without speaking a word. All three dogs, curled up at the foot of the bed, watched. He floated out of the room as the sparklers went out.

His consciousness, soul, or spirit had come to visit her, to let her know everything was all right.

THE OLDEST MAN

In 2014 a friend of mine, Polish-born Dr. Alexander Imich, passed away. At the time of his death, he was the oldest man in the United States and the second-oldest man in the world. Dr. Imich had survived the Russian gulags and had powerful afterlife communications. Though he had a doctorate in zoology, he had eventually gravitated toward chemistry. Science fascinated him. He was also a parapsychologist, president of the Anomalous Phenomena Research Center in New York City, and dedicated most of his 111 years of life to investigating life-after-death experiences.

Imich loved conversation and was very open with me about his life, his losses, and beliefs. He told me his beloved wife, Wela, had passed in 1986 and that this loss had devastated him. Imich and Wela never had children, but their life was still very full. She had been a gifted painter and psychotherapist. As our friendship grew, I saw he had an incredible sense of humor and was very engaged in living, especially for someone who had survived such a difficult youth.

I'd initially contacted him when I was working on one of my books. I knew about him through my literary agent, and I wanted to ask him what the secret was to his long life. Imich, who had reconnected to his own Judaism just before he passed, replied, "Have passion and stay involved in something you really care about, which has meaning for you." After reading some of his works, I realized we had similar interests, but research wise he was way ahead of the curve.

When he died, I understood why he had to wait a century to begin putting on tefillin (phylacteries containing Torah verses, worn during prayer). Imich hadn't participated in this tradition since he was a bar mitzvah. Witnessing and experiencing harsh, brutal treatment during the Holocaust or in gulag camps often created a wedge, separating such individuals from Judaism, and for decades Imich had been no different.

Though he backed away from the religion of his youth, this didn't keep him from exploring an afterlife. He talked about how he had received a "kiss" from a spirit person and confessed it was an agreeable experience. In a 2012 blog about Imich for White Crow Books, author Michael Tymn wrote that Imich "says that 'communications from and appearances of deceased people' have been the major phenomena leading to his belief that consciousness survives death." Such spiritual experiences were the foundation for his lack of fear of death. He had a strong certainty that consciousness survives.

Imich was a true force to be reckoned with. Living on his own in an apartment in Manhattan and still writing, there was no sitting on the couch for this guy. In his nineties he'd published two books and numerous articles. Imich told me he meditated, exercised daily, didn't smoke or drink alcohol, and had a very healthy diet. His mind was always clear and sharp.

When I asked if he was a Holocaust survivor, he didn't hold back. In 1939 he and his wife, Wela, were in Soviet Russia. With Stalin in power, accepted ideas about humanity and humane treatment took a turn for the worst. One major shift in thinking was the ethnic cleansing or Russification of non-Russians. Because of this Imich spent several years in degrading, subfreezing Russian concentration camps.

My husband's grandfather, Samuel, did business in Volkovysk, Poland (now Belarus). When the Nazis invaded, he tried to cross the Lithuanian border and was picked up by the Russians. Being Jewish, Samuel too was also promptly sent to a gulag. He reclaimed his spirituality in his later years. The loss of dignity and extreme slave labor was difficult for both men, but they survived.

After refusing Soviet citizenship, Imich and his wife were sent by boxcar train to a gulag near the White Sea. It took blood, sweat, tears, and even death to build the White Sea–Baltic Canal. There were over a hundred thousand prisoners at camp Belbaltlag, and they became Stalin's forced labor for building this waterway. The price for this was the tragic deaths of too many.

In August 1933 a dramatic performance was carefully lined out for dignitaries visiting Belbaltlag. The day-to-day brutality prisoners experienced was hidden from the group of one hundred and twenty Russian writers and artists. This so-called Writers Brigade, which included Maxim Gorky, Aleksey Nikolayevich Tolstoy, and others, published their findings at the end of 1934. Viktor Shklovsky and Mikhail Zoshchenko compiled a 600-page monograph applauding the project called *The I.V. Stalin White Sea—Baltic Sea Canal* (Russian: Беломорско-Балтийский канал имени Сталина).

During his imprisonment, Imich had no information about the well-being of his family or their whereabouts. Once out of the death camp, he discovered a tragic truth: many friends and relatives had not survived the Holocaust.

Unlike some survivors returning from the camps, he not only talked openly about his experiences, but also turned his energies toward his previous passion, investigating consciousness and life after physical death. When asked about his own eventual passing, he replied, in a 2014 interview with the *New York Times* by Ralph Blumenthal, that "the compensation for dying is that I will learn all the things I was not able to learn here on Earth."

Imich says in his book, *Incredible Tales of the Paranormal:* "Imagine for a moment how much human life would change if this question were answered in the positive, how much easier it would be to live through the pain and misery of our existence on this planet, if we were sure, these were only temporary ills."

As a well-respected scientist and researcher, he tried to convince his peers in the scientific community that consciousness continues after the physical body dies. During our conversations, I quickly realized Imich knew we all had a spirit, soul, or light that survived physical death.

In a Newser article by Rob Quinn, Imich's lifelong friend, Michael Mannion, reported that days before his death in Manhattan, New York, Imich was "speaking Polish and Russian to spirits (those who had proceeded him in death) he felt were around him."

There is a purpose in sharing Imich's extraordinary story. By introducing you to a rigorous modern-day scientist who survived horrific tragedy in his early years, we can learn a valuable lesson. We see in talking without reservation about his losses, Imich reclaimed his dignity. Then for the rest of his long life, he continued to be one of the prominent pioneers in afterlife research.

Though he lost most of his family to the Holocaust, he did make peace with a god of his understanding and his Jewish tradition. Because Imich made peace with himself and his history, he was also able to open the door for many researchers, including myself.

LET'S LOOK AT THE NUMBERS

What impact did Hitler and Stalin have on the spirituality of the Jewish people? We can get a hint if we are willing to research. I love looking at polls. Trends in society have always fascinated me. That said, I'm cautious about political or news polls during an election. Every pollster seems to have a different set of numbers based on their own political slant. I'm just as careful when exploring religious traditions and the belief in life after death.

An August 2018 Pew Research Center report ("The Religious Typology") examined the religious beliefs of the U.S. population, conducting a survey among 4,729 members of the center's American Trends Panel. The respondents were divided into three broad categories: highly religious (39 percent of respondents), somewhat religious (32 percent), and nonreligious (29 percent). Among American Jews, nearly half (45 percent) considered themselves nonreligious. The nonreligious were further divided into "Religion Resisters," who think organized religion is harmful but usually still have a belief in a higher power, to "Solidly Secular," who hold no religious beliefs whatsoever. About half of the latter identified as atheists.

A Pew Research Center survey conducted earlier that year determined that a majority of Jews do, however, have a belief in a higher power (Dalia Fahmy, "Key Findings about American's Belief in God"). It showed that 89 percent of American Jews believe in God, compared to 99 percent of Christians. High percentages in polls can have different meanings, but an 89 percent acceptance in God is a strong number for any survey. Looking at a recognition of God may not be about a return to the god of ancient literature. Instead, rebuilding some sort of trust in a higher power, the universe, or a god of one's choosing could be responsible for this high number.

What is interesting about surveys on Jewish afterlife beliefs is how contradictory they can be. Interestingly, as I've perused polls, I found a belief in God doesn't necessarily translate into an acceptance of an afterlife. Life after death is rarely discussed within prominent branches of Judaism, but what's curious is most of the Jewish community believes in God or some form of a higher power. Looking at research, we see this belief has even increased over the last few decades. The confusion is this conviction doesn't match up with Jewish afterlife beliefs.

In comparison to this when we look at the percentage of those who believe in the afterlife, the number is much lower, though growing. A 2000 *Washington Post* article by Richard Morin cited statistics indicating that the belief has been increasing: "belief in life after death is growing among Jews, according to data collected in the General Social Survey conducted annually by the University of Chicago's National Opinion Research Center. In the 1970s, 19 percent of Jews said they believed in life after death. Twenty years later, 56 percent said they believed in an afterlife."

To confuse matters, 2014 research by the Pew Research Center (published in a 2015 article by Caryle Murphy) shows us only 40 percent of Jews believe in heaven or, in Hebrew, Olam Ha-Ba, which translates as the "world to come." Though there is a belief in a Jewish afterlife, less than half of the population embraces this. The Holocaust and atrocities of the Soviet Union turned the comfort of past spirituality upside down. So many of those who were impacted by these horrible years lost their faith and, most important, trust. Is the situation hopeless? I don't think so. A few years ago, I had a debate with a researcher about Jewish afterlife views. One of my responses was:

> The afterlife is not forgotten by the Jews. It was just put on a back burner. Tradition says the mission of focusing in on life, and then helping the Jewish people survive will always take a front row seat. For everything there is a season and the afterlife has its place. After what happened in Nazi Germany, and Russia, along with centuries of persecution this is the way it is. Caution must always be used when

discussing the Jews and an afterlife. Always remember the answer isn't always cut and dry. It's very Jewish and very complicated.

What we have seen is after World War II officially ended in 1945, the belief in life after death was extremely low. With so many losses of family, friends, home, possessions, health, and dignity, faith in spiritual well-being, trust, and security was very compromised. Twenty years later, the numbers doubled. Spirituality is returning. With each generation, hope may be on the rise.

SIX

The Effect of PTSD on Faith in the Jewish Community

A man who cannot survive bad times, will not see good times.

—HASSIDIC JEWISH PROVERB

When anyone goes through traumatic events there will be consequences. How one reacts to such consequences determines whether recovery can happen. When survivors believe that sharing will be hurtful and upsetting to family and friends, they create one more unrealistic fear.

Mothers or fathers suffering from untreated trauma or sexual exploitation can pass their unresolved terror, shame, and self-destructive tendencies to their children. Though these children may not have been traumatized or molested, they can look like survivors of abuse. There is a reason for this. How can an abused parent who has not received help model health when he or she has been so damaged? Intervention must happen.

THE TRAUMATIC LEGACY OF
THE HOLOCAUST

Sadly, after World War II survivors of the Holocaust didn't initially open up about their horrific experiences with family, friends, religious communities, or neighbors. I didn't know my aunt's detailed history in the camps until she was in her early eighties. Her full account was shared when we were in Auschwitz. A trip to Ukraine for a big family wedding introduced me to cousins who provided me with details about man-made famines, slave camps, gulags, and other atrocities in Russia. My grandparents never discussed our family saga in Siberia or Kazakhstan. Unfortunately, it's difficult to experience healthy spirituality if we are not airing out the tragedies of the past. My grandmother's tragedies taught her to fear death.

Because of persecution, man-made famines, murders, and the gulags, four of my great-grandparents left Russia. They and their ancestors had lived along this waterway for nearly three hundred years. Here they had prospered, turning desolate land, on which murderous nomadic tribes once roamed, into a breadbasket of agriculture and prosperity. Beginning in 1871 Russification was on the rise. Successful individuals who were not of Russian ancestry were now seen as *kulaks,* uppity peasants with farms and businesses. The Russian crown was convinced it was their right to take wealth away from those who had created it.

My great-grandparents came to this country leaving relatives behind, and they rarely mentioned where they had come from. I remember one of my great-grandfathers always being somewhat depressed. Even as a little girl, I thought he was a sad man. Despite his losses he rolled up his sleeves and started work laboring in vineyards. Eventually, he was able to buy his own land, and his tasty grapes continue to grow today. Every time I see a box or bag of California raisins, I know where they come from. Though he had achieved the American dream, emotionally tragedy followed him.

When I got older, I tried to ask one of my great aunts about the old country. She was always reluctant to speak about those times. This spunky woman who was a butcher by profession and had lived to be 102 years old did finally tell me a bit about the family. Much of what she told me didn't resonate with family health and wellness. For me, these red flags for past unresolved trauma were easy to see.

My great-grandfather used alcohol to medicate his feelings. He could become very violent or suffer bouts of depression. In several instances he was institutionalized in sanatoriums. Most of his family members were left behind in Russia and never heard from again. The survivor's guilt he must have felt knowing many of his loved ones had perished so brutally must have been enormous. During his times of emotional outburst, my great-grandmother would retreat. I heard he would chase her around with a kitchen knife. A very kind person, she could not deal with conflict. To this day I know very little about her family, and I'm not sure how many of them survived persecution.

My father's mother, my grandmother, was like her mother. She was a kind person who was there for me whenever I needed her, but she had a hard time taking a stance about conflicts or concerns, and any form of family scuffle was difficult for her. There were lots of secrets between her and my grandfather, but these were rarely aired. My grandmother also had a habit of withdrawing when she felt uncomfortable. Because of this people would say she was distant or a snob. I ended up carrying these same characteristics. There was a time when I would become very uncomfortable at gatherings. Feeling myself fading into the woodwork, I'd retreat into my own little world. Some of those around me would interpret this as haughty behavior.

My father followed his father's sad journey. Though successful and active with community service endeavors, emotionally part of him was numb and empty. The only obvious emotion was rage and depression. One minute he was the life of the party and someone to be admired for his achievements. The next moment he could be throwing dishes across the room. He is not alone.

A successful business owner and Holocaust survivor, he worked hard at repressing his rage. Unfortunately, the bottled-up emotion leaked out. With hidden secrets about past sufferings, the children, grandchildren, and even great-grandchildren of a survivor can find themselves in spiritual retreat. To understand these behaviors, it was central for me to begin looking not only at my family history, but also at whose emotional journey I was unconsciously following.

One summer I decided to get together with some of my cousins. None of us had ever talked about our upbringing. As we sat chatting about our own children, conversations turned to our parents, grandparents, and great-grandparents. The similar traumas, confusion, fear, and depression we all shared caught me completely off guard. I realized most of my cousins had grown up with parents plagued with anger, sadness, or fear, so I wasn't crazy or alone.

As I sat there, I realized all of us had suffered similar abuses growing up. Free-floating emotions plagued the lot of us, not just me and my family.

My journey then expanded into really looking at the past and how this had hurt so many of us. After I spoke with my cousins, I soon realized we were each carrying family feelings without knowing it. The feelings at the bottom of these secrets about what happened in Russia were not going to be buried, ignored, or push away. Though not directly experienced, these losses were tied to emotions we all now felt. When they surfaced, it could be overwhelming, leaving us with feelings of despair, worthlessness, uncertainty, fear of sanity, and distress from experiences that were never ours.

Bonds between family and friends can be a blessing or a curse. Though unresolved emotions tied to past family loss can disrupt our lives, it's our job to unravel this confusion. In doing this we can then see how we are bonded to those who came before us.

The Trauma of Veterans and Holocaust Survivors

Damage is damage and accepting this can help remove the stigma PTSD currently carries. According to data posted on the U.S. Department of Veterans Affairs website, here are the following estimated numbers for identified occurrence of PTSD in just those who serve in the U.S. military.

Thirty out of a hundred Vietnam veterans have reported PTSD symptoms.

For Desert Storm veterans, ten out of a hundred report PTSD issues.

Of those vets returning from Afghanistan, as high as eleven out of a hundred reported PTSD symptoms.

Around twenty out of a hundred vets returning from the Iraq war have shared PTSD symptoms.

Personally and professionally, I believe the numbers are a lot higher. There is still a great deal of shame when it comes to talking about war experiences. Like those who suffered during the Holocaust or gulags during the Lenin and Stalin years, the no-talk rule continues to be in play.

PTSD in returning vets is often missed for a variety of reasons.

Vets don't recognize current living problems could be linked to past military experiences.

They don't ask for help, believing it's a sign of weakness.

They won't tell physicians, therapists, or psychologists the true state of their being.

They can't see when their behavior or reactions are over the top and extreme.

Consciously or unconsciously, they work to deny symptoms.

They can be functional but then experience drastic mood swings.

Their behavior is often misdiagnosed as antisocial, and PTSD is missed.

Excessive drug or alcohol use can mask PTSD symptoms.

During exit interviews with the armed forces at the end of their tours, any PTSD symptoms are denied or minimized.

The PTSD symptoms of other trauma survivors are also masked or missed in similar ways.

After the trauma that occurred during the Hitler and Stalin years, survivors and offspring worked at forgetting those events. Survivors with unresolved history will work consciously or unconsciously to deny or hide the past. They may not realize how it is impacting their current lives or that their current problems are tied to losses in the past. Among the problems they encounter are:

They are ashamed of asking for help with memories and experiences related to the past.

Survivors don't share with doctors or therapists the extent of their history and trauma.

Helping professionals may misdiagnose their trauma as mental illness or strictly psychological.

Though they can function and even be extremely successful, they still suffer bouts of mood swings.

They have issues with overwork and eating problems.

Prescription drugs or alcohol maybe used to mask feelings about the past.

The pattern and similarities between military personnel who watched their buddies die gruesome deaths on battlefields and survivors who witnessed loved ones being gassed, starved, shot, or hanged are obvious. Over the years I've worked with World War II, Korean,

Vietnam, Desert Storm, Enduring Freedom, and Iraqi Freedom vets, along with prisoners of war, Holocaust survivors and their families, and the children, grandchildren, and great-grandchildren of Nazis. In many of these cases most survivors of trauma were unaware they were suffering from this PTSD. Such lack of cognizance is not uncommon.

LONG-TERM EFFECTS OF CHILD ABUSE

There are many after-effects to another form of trauma—child abuse. If childhood sexual abuse is not treated, long-term symptoms can go on through adulthood. From the National Center for PTSD, here are a few consequences to such damage:

PTSD and anxiety
Depression and thoughts of suicide, self-harm
Sexual anxiety and disorders, including having too many or unsafe
    sexual partners
Difficulty setting safe limits with others and relationship problems
Poor body image and low self-esteem
Alcoholism and drug abuse
Eating problems

These behaviors are often used to hide painful emotions related to the abuse.

Parents who were mistreated as children often don't talk about their abuse, thinking they are sparing their children from heartache. When current situations and events pull up unwanted memories of past trauma, behavior for these adults can change. Intense feelings can be overwhelming. Victims who are now adults may:

Feel isolated
Feel emotionally numb

Have unexplained fears

Struggle with depression

Experience sexual issues

Encounter relationship difficulties

These parents can also be at risk for over parenting their offspring. Children won't understand what is going on with Mom or Dad, but they will feel it. Like little spongers they can absorb their parents' unresolved feelings. Once adults get help, they are less likely to pass these emotions on to their children.

In some cases, suicide and self-destruction can be a consequence of being in or witnessing life-threatening situations. A survivor can only diminish his or her suffering if assistance of some sort is sought out. Once this happens, the no-talk rule dies, and we are free to embrace ourselves and our true destiny, our spirituality, and our creativity.

PTSD of Holocaust Survivors

Studies show us how Holocaust survivors can also suffer post-traumatic stress. How often I've heard from survivors: "How could God let this happen?" "Where was God when my entire family was murdered?" With this unresolved rage at all things spiritual, any form of afterlife encounter will be pushed to the side. The consequences of silence don't serve their families but instead can create a host of concerns. These feelings can seep downward through the family tree, producing struggles with the self and spirituality. Some survivors did not talk to their children about their Holocaust experiences. This second generation were raised in homes of hidden mystery, and the silence contributed to a culture of repression within these families. Based on my work with families of the Holocaust, I've seen difficulties not only for the first generation, but also the second, third, fourth, and even fifth generations.

Just how bad has it been for these silent survivors? It can be quite damaging. In the early 2000s, doctors at the Abarbanel Mental Health Center in Bat-Yam, Israel, which is affiliated with the Sackler School of Medicine, Tel Aviv University, conducted a study to assess whether elderly Holocaust survivors were at increased risk of suicide. They published their findings in the August 2005 issue of the *American Journal of Geriatric Psychiatry* (Y. Barak et al., "Increased Risk of Attempted Suicide among Aging Holocaust Survivors"). The researchers found that 24 percent of Abarbanel patients who were Holocaust survivors had tried to commit suicide, compared with only 8.2 percent of the patients who were not survivors (general population).

A study, published in 2016, that looked into the long-term prognosis of Holocaust survivors with acute myocardial infarction, discovered that these survivors had similar and even slightly better survival rates than the general population. However, the researchers (Arthur Shiyovich et al.) found a higher prevalence of depression in this group, which itself is associated with a nearly 78 percent increased risk for mortality.

Six hundred Holocaust survivors were assessed for PTSD by medical experts in a long-term study. The findings of the researchers, Harald Freyberger and Hellmuth Freyberger, validated concerns about survivors. They concluded in their study, which they published in a 2007 article, that "in more than the half of the patients . . . [t]he most frequent posttraumatic stress disorder symptoms were sleep disturbances, recurrent nightmares, intrusive recollections as well as depressive and anxiety disorders." In an earlier study, published in 1992, researchers K. Kutch and B. J. Cox found that "most survivors had not received adequate psychiatric care."

TREATING PTSD

In my clinical practice, I have been working with PTSD sufferers and their families for over thirty-five years. Successful treatment for PTSD involves several therapeutic steps.

1. Debriefing the traumatic experiences—sharing the story.
2. Connecting to the strong emotions of the experience and processing those feelings and memories in a safe and appropriate manner.
3. Integrating the extreme life-threatening event into the total life experience with the grieving process.
4. Developing a spiritual side that works.

Again, any sufferer who does not properly sort out his or her past suffering risks passing unresolved emotions onto children and/or spouses. If survivors have issues with death, dying, or afterlife encounters, their offspring will also have similar difficulties. As time moves on, the ability to repress emotion can become more difficult. Because of this, strong feelings related to original devastating experiences can be misdirected onto current life events. Displaced anger; sadness; guilt; or feelings of failure, loss, or fear can be transferred onto marriages, in parenting children (see my book *Learning to Say No: Establishing Healthy Boundaries*), with friends, job situations, or other life happenings. Initially, feelings of agitation, anxiety, mild depression, or frustration can surface before the eruption of core feelings like grief, terror, and rage. This unconscious release of emotion is not usually purposeful. It's a reaction to "triggers."

Triggers in the here and now—such as newspaper articles reporting pain or loss or incidences about the days of Hitler and Stalin, radio or television reports, smells, movies, and a host of other environmental stimuli—can pull from the past overwhelming, strong bodily sensations and hidden emotion. Such reactions are not only confusing and overwhelming for the sufferer but also for family members. Children, grandchildren, and spouses can personalize such reactions and make these extreme emotional outbursts or distancing behavior about them. Past sorrow can make embracing afterlife contacts, hearing about them, or reading of such events difficult to say the least. We may each need to walk a different path to accomplish taming our triggers. Hopefully, we can now see why it's up to the survivors—the second, third, or even fourth generations—to become educated about the symptoms of such great loss and sorrow.

FILLING OUR HOLES

Some Holocaust survivors find peace in their synagogues and rabbis and by associating with other survivors. Others branch off into creativity or pour their energies into their families and building businesses. Being a helpful member of society is top of the list. These individuals also tend to talk about their experiences and share how they continue to heal.

Holocaust survivor and artist Alice Lok Cahana was born in Budapest, Hungry. Before she passed, I had the privilege of meeting her on several occasions. Her process of opening up about her experiences allowed other survivors to come forward and do the same.

After the war and liberation, Cahana became a well-known artist living in Houston, Texas. Her work even had a showing at Auschwitz. With strokes of paint moving from dark to light, she was able to depict not only the horrors of the Holocaust, but also her journey thereafter. Through her paintings she broke the no-talk rule about her past. Along with being very public about her losses, Cahana's canvases give us hope and a powerful message. In a catalog about her artwork shown in a traveling exhibition curated by Barbara Gilbert (*From Ashes to the Rainbow: A Tribute to Raoul Wallenberg*), Cahana had this to say about her work:

> I made a painting that has holes in it. Why are there holes? Because God says to us, I cannot do all. I can create you, but I cannot do it all. You have to help Me fix the holes and put everything together. This is the learning from the Holocaust. That each of us is here to fix the holes.

We all have holes in our life in need of our full attention. If we still follow a no-talk rule and have had an afterlife contact we have not shared with others, we are at risk of missing the message. Without healing we will be less willing to embrace the meaning of life, here and now, today and with a world of any sort to come. Instead, we might find ourselves dismissing or even snickering at those who have had similar experiences. Our anger and grief will keep us from seeing.

Even though I didn't directly experience the persecutions of my ancestors, their hidden emotional wounds were still passed on down to me. As a young girl I'd had numerous departing visions but refused to acknowledge them. Instead, I looked angrily upon any form of spirituality, trying my best to ignore these precious events. For me *god* was a curse word for several decades. If the word was mentioned, rage and hate would immediately surface and bury me in overwhelming emotion. The undealt with tragedies of those who came before me had manifested into dreadful abuse, and I'd become a victim. My family members hadn't talked about their history, and I wasn't going to discuss mine anytime soon.

I could have stayed bitter and angry at the world. Instead, I listened to the survivors around me and eventually got the memo. The feelings I'd inherited from members of my family, along with my own unresolved emotions were eating me alive from the inside out. I needed to realize that unlike the generations before me, I hadn't been locked in a prison. Regardless of our past we still have choices.

Spiritual evolution is what living life is all about. It took me fifteen years to forgive those who had intentionally or unintentionally hurt me. I'm not saying it was easy, but it was my responsibility. At times I even felt suicidal. Instead of cutting myself short on my own journey, I returned to the hopeful words of those around me, "You are responsible. With our help you can fix yourself."

In her article "Life after Death," Sara Yoheved Rigler, prolific writer on Jewish spirituality, wrote that being alive on Earth is like winning the "Supermarket Jackpot." It's an opportunity to fix ourselves and the world that we mustn't squander:

> This World has one (and only one!) advantage over the other worlds: This is the only world where the soul can change, grow, and elevate itself. . . . the choice between right and wrong, good and evil is ours. Every time we chose [*sic*] honesty over cheating, generosity over selfishness, or faithfulness over betrayal, we refine ourselves. By consistently choosing good over evil, we make ourselves into the refined beings who can enjoy the Light of the Divine Presence in the World of Truth. . . . Judaism mourns death because it cuts short the opportunity to fix oneself in This World.

Survivors like Alice Lok Cahana recognized no God destroyed their families. No angry God stood by and let suffering happen. After her release from the camps, she had to stand up and let the world know, "I'm still here." Humankind, each one of us, has some measure of free will. With the roll of the dice, we can find ourselves happy or depressed, confident, or tormented, excited, or terrified. If we have loss or carry past pain, we must do the work necessary, for however long it takes, to heal. We must release all buried emotions while in a safe place, with safe people and share our stories of survival. Many who suffered through the desperate times of World War II, along with its consequences to the following generations, have done this. Using our own innate sense of spirituality to overcome bitterness, shame, and fear we can proudly share with the world, "I am not a victim. I'm a survivor."

Years ago, I met Diane LaRoe, a very vivacious woman. She had found my request for near-death accounts I had placed in a circular and contacted me. Though I never knew for sure what her Jewish heritage was, she appeared very open to all religions. Having studied voice at Juilliard School of Music, she was a most creative, open-minded soul. When she passed in 2005, I knew we had lost a bright shard of brilliance. LaRoe's extraordinary account drives home what spiritual evolution might look like. Outside of her experiences with a morgue—yes, I said morgue—most of her encounters and messages are like those found in historic Jewish afterlife accounts. Below is a great example of finding one's true purpose in life, an account she shared with me during an interview. Look for the similarities.

I Woke Up in a Morgue
Diane LaRoe

Many years ago, I was killed as a result of an automobile accident. The ambulance doctor pinned a DOA sign on my coat and delivered me to the Santa Monica morgue.

While I was dead, I heard a voice ask if I wanted to stay where I was forever. I knew this was the Omnipotent Power talking, and I answered, as quickly as I could, yes. I felt so protected, safe, and really at home. It was the perfect place to be. I'd never been so happy. I just surrendered.

While on the other side I was taught about the blessings, powers, and gifts we humans were given because we are loved. I learned we could heal ourselves and others, contact those on Earth as well as those who had crossed over, and conduct this service for others. God told me I had to return to this plane and tell everyone how to find and use these powers.

I wrote a book—The Awakening—making sure all know there is no such thing as death. It is just a transmission from one plane to another.

An Awakening and Blessing

When we let go of the no-talk rule, our progression will continue. Enlightenment happens, and we begin to see things differently while gaining new perspective. Life will take us on a path full of new knowledge, interesting challenges, relationships, broader understanding, and creativity. We need no longer push away our own afterlife contacts or those of others. We can finally start to accept that reunions with those deceased generations who came before us just might be possible. In doing this we now have choices in how to respond. Passing these accounts onto the younger generation just might put a stop to continued death phobia. In doing this the fear of death and carried feelings from previous life difficulties can be softened.

Reading through these pages my hope is we are recognizing how we Jews have not been banned from any spiritual opportunity or opening. We have also seen how unaddressed loss and grief can keep this porthole clouded. To bring in a ray of spiritual sunshine we must honestly take stock of ourselves and discover where we've come from. Bandages will no longer work. We must dig deep to mend the whole wound.

Beginning such a journey helps us to become open to afterlife encounters. With this we then build up our own sense of personal consciousness. If we can hear ourselves speak of our secrets, we can then hear about life after death. In doing this the fear of death begins to fade. We can then openly share with others what we've learned about universes much greater than our current physical situation.

Most important, our children, grandchildren and great-grandchildren will not be as confounded as we have been because of history and the emotions tied to it. They will experience more freedom from fears, depression, and confusion.

> *And whoever saves a life, it is considered as if he saved an entire world.*
>
> —MISHNAH, SANHEDRIN 4:5

By embracing the totality of who we are and where we have come from, in disbanding concerns about physical death, we will be healing not only the past and present, but also healing generations to come.

SEVEN

Facing Our Ancestral Past to Heal Future Generations

Oh, the tree of life is growing
Where the spirit never dies
And the bright light of salvation shines
In dark and empty skies
—Bob Dylan, from "Death Is Not the End"

Bob Dylan has been an icon for many generations. A creative genius who's paved the way not only for upcoming musicians but also for anyone listening. At times his lyrics have sounded like anarchy or an anthem for social justice. For a number of us who grew up during the turbulent 1960s, Dylan's words helped grow our sense of consciousness and are imprinted upon our souls. Today, his messages about communal awareness and mindfulness continue to be a useful road map.

Bob Dylan's real name is Robert Allen Zimmerman. According to a 2005 article by Nadine Epstein and Rebecca Frankel, detailing Dylan's early life and religious upbringing, his father, Abe Zimmerman, grew up with parents who had immigrated to the United States from Eastern Europe. In 1907 Abe's parents, Dylan's grandparents, Zigman and Anna Zimmerman, arrived from Russia, or what is now known as Ukraine. Persecution had made Jews outcasts in their own homes. Many were murdered, and their livelihoods stolen, creating great poverty and starvation. Dylan spent his very Jewish childhood in a predominantly Jewish community. During this time his father, Abe, was overcome with polio. In the 1950s the family then moved to Hibbing, Minnesota, another Jewish community. Here Dylan's father served as president of B'nai Brith synagogue, and his beautiful mother, Beatty, took a turn as head of the Hadassah group. Beatty's mother and father were from Lithuania. In the late 1800s and early 1900s, pogroms and anti-Semitism forced many Jews to flee from Lithuania. Though Dylan appears to have had a traditional conservative Jewish upbringing, within a very Jewish society, with Sabbat services, Torah study, a bar mitzvah, and trips to summer camp, the oppression of the generations before him created a period of spiritual confusion. In his quest for answers he even converted to Christianity. With memories of tyranny so ingrained in his ancestors, this could explain why Dylan has been such a trailblazer for the rights of the downtrodden and exploited. In attempting to liberate people, I believe he felt that he had not received a fair shake in life; he just might have been trying to sort out his own sense of spiritual confusion.

"Neighborhood Bully," one of Dylan's 1980s ballads, not only looks at Judaism's past but also at Israel's current place in the world. Within the ballad's lyrics we get a sense of how Dylan might have struggled with his heritage. In a 2018 interview with Barry Shrage—Brandeis University professor and former president of Combined Jewish Philanthropies—about Dylan's ballad, Shrage notes that "when he [Dylan] said he has no place to run to, no place to go, it's sort of a reference to the Holocaust. In other words, when the Jewish people are in trouble, they literally have no place to run to and no place to go."

In 1997 Dylan put together a new album called *Time Out of Mind*. The project began shortly after his friend Jerry Garcia—singer, songwriter, and Grateful Dead band spokesperson—died from a heart attack in 1995. In reviewing the words on this work I believe Dylan had become jaded by the music industry and was also confronting his own physical impermanence and place in the world. Using his spiritual creativity, he tapped into his music to review where he had traveled in life. He also explored how he was emotionally struggling with his current place in the universe and what immortality meant to him. I believe with this venture he began to find answers.

HELPFUL MESSAGES FROM
THE AFTERLIFE

When Dylan was just sixteen, he saw the popular 1950s rock-'n'-roller Buddy Holly play in concert. He was mesmerized and felt an instant connection with the songster. In 1959, just three days after Dylan's encounter with this musical genius, Holly, along with other well-known artists, died tragically in a plane crash. Holly's unique rockabilly style has since influenced Dylan's music throughout his career. While Dylan was recording *Time Out of Mind*, Holly's spirit seemed to be there, at his side and everywhere he went. In a 1998 interview with Murray Engleheart for *Guitar World*, he talked about his experiences:

> While we were recording, every place I turned there was Buddy Holly. . . . Every place you turned. You walked down a hallway and you heard Buddy Holly records, like "That'll Be the Day." Then you'd get in the car to go over to the studio and "Rave On" would be playing. Then you'd walk into this studio and someone's playing a cassette of "It's So Easy." And this would happen day after day after day. Phrases of Buddy Holly songs would just come out of

nowhere. It was spooky. [laughs] . . . Buddy Holly's spirit must have been someplace, hastening this record.

This sounds like an after-death communication to me. Before he recorded the music for this album, Dylan had been in a difficult spot professionally, artistically, and personally. Holly might just have come to his rescue by making his presence known.

The last time I saw Dylan was in the coastal town of Santa Cruz, California. When I was young this was a popular destination and retreat for members of my family. The sea, mist, sand, and sun are so very healing. Sitting on the pier, taking in the sights, smells, and music, meditation is easy. I might even receive a vision. Seeing the web of life, connecting every living creature, rock, plant, air, wind, and other universes, reminds me I'm never alone. And with Dylan on the beach, I definitely wasn't by myself!

Staying in a wonderful hotel located right off the blue ocean, just down the street from a place my grandparents made our summer getaway, I caught a glimpse of Bob Dylan. Dressed in all black and surrounded by roadies, his fans crowded the lobby. Though he had changed a bit physically, the themes for his music were just the same. As I continued to take in the scene, I wondered how many of Dylan's devoted followers knew at one time he had been so emotionally confused and bewildered about his own spirit. Their hero had struggled when it came to his private sense of spirituality.

At times we think we are the only ones struggling, but like me and so many of us, Dylan the poet and seer had searched for his personal prophet for decades. Trying to navigate life and discover what spirituality truly is has taken Dylan on many twists and turns. Researching his journey, he's bounced from one religion to another and back again. Taking the time to really investigate what's out there takes work and time and involves a great deal of self-reflection. We must make peace with who we are if we are going to discover our own awareness of spirituality. Saying this I must also add, to learn from our exploration, patience is necessary.

Dylan's continued spiritual evolution is the result of his creativity. Intergenerational emotions related to the traumas of Russia were examined and healed with poetry, social action, and song. One doesn't need to see a burning bush to experience the mysteries of life and heal. Look up at the brilliance of the multitude of stars in the night sky and know there really is something much greater out there. Each of us has a few skeletons in the closet. We all have things we don't like about ourselves, but the stars will not disappear because of this. When we can look closely at ourselves, our history, past grief issues and losses, we spiritually evolve. This then frees us up to step away from the no-talk rule.

Becoming more interested in looking into our spiritual nature we see that with creativity, not just the artist, but the homemaker, musician, physician, railroad worker, writer, cook, dancer, singer, mechanic, politician, person of service, parents, and grandparents can make the world a better place. All of us can explore our own different path while still making a difference. Like Dylan, we too can find meaning to our lives.

Bob Dylan's after-death communication with Buddy Holly hopefully showed him that he was never alone. The encounter may have even precipitated a philosophical change of heart about life. He's not the only one to have afterlife assistance.

More than a decade ago I met a man who told me about receiving visits and messages from deceased friends and family. Because of his encounters he didn't fear death. Instead, he could direct his energies toward living life. I recounted his experiences in my 2014 blog for White Crow Books.

I am a Jewish male, age 72, who has had these "visitations" for many years. It is not uncommon for relatives and friends who are deceased to "visit" with me. Sometimes they deliver messages and sometimes they are just there. Also, many times I am awakened during the night, sit up in bed and see these "forms" moving around the room.

These messages are called after-death contacts. As we will see in the following story, such experiences relieved this man of any fear of death. Several years later he shared with me the following account.

An Update from an Older Jewish Gentleman

I have had several heart surgeries and a major heart attack. While I was in intensive care after one of my surgeries, I had a visitation that might be of interest to you. At the time, I was neither depressed nor afraid of dying.

To give you a little background, my best friend for over sixty years died last year after a prolonged illness. His story is a tragic one. He was predeceased by both of his children and his wife. His life was frequently compared to that of Job in the Bible.

I was asleep in intensive care, and in my dreams, I saw a river. One side was very dark, and the other was extremely bright. The bright side was beautiful, with green grass and rolling hills. I was on the dark side. Suddenly, my friend and his wife appeared with one of their children on the bright side of the river. He and his wife were holding hands and all of them were smiling and laughing. My mother and father (both deceased) also appeared smiling, laughing, and waving. A little boy was with them. I realized I had previously seen this child. I believe the boy to be my grandson who died at childbirth.

My maternal grandmother and one of my maternal aunts were also there, smiling, laughing, and waving. My friend from the other side of the river spoke to me and said, "When the time comes, my wife and I will take you across the river." I awoke, not frightened, but kind of peaceful. As I said I was not afraid of dying before the visitation and certainly not afterward.

Having made peace with encounters of this nature, this experiencer learned he would not die alone. His family and friends in an afterlife existence would be there for him when his time came. Based on his visions he might have even received a brief peek at where he would be going after he left this life. Before experiencing my own departing visions, I would have scoffed at the above stories. Today, hearing these same words daily from people of all walks of life still astonishes me. The above encounters once again show us that interaction between our physical world and the afterlife happens. Death of the material body doesn't dissolve loving relationships.

With bonds of love remaining unbroken from one generation to the next, family connections can stay strong. Even when relationships are difficult, we can't ignore how we've been influenced by those who have crossed our path. With difficult relationships there can still be a tie of sorts. To deny this is to reject our own sense of connection to one another and ourselves. By refusing to look at current or past links, we are denying part of our very own existence.

What follows is a dialogue I've constructed from the many comments I've heard over the years from everyday Jewish afterlife experiencers around the world.

"I had the most amazing experience."

"Oh really? I'd love to hear about it."

"Yes, I think you're the only person I can share this with."

"Why is that? Is everything in your life all right?"

"As incredible as this experience was, it also changed my view of the world. Everything is turned upside down. It's made me really look at who I am, and my place in the cosmos! The meaning of my life isn't what I thought it was. It's so much more."

"Sounds life changing. I'd love to know the details of your experience."

"Well, when I had open heart surgery, I felt myself lifting up out of my body. Then I had the sensation there were others around me who had already died."

"Was this scary or upsetting?

"No! It felt wonderful. I saw my grandparents and a brother who had died years ago."

"Did they say anything to you?

"We talked a bit, but it was mind to mind."

"How did they look, appear?"

"They seemed great, even my older brother who was so sick all of the time."

"Why was he sick?"

"As a kid I really loved playing with him, but then he developed problems with his heart. He grew weaker and weaker and eventually was bedridden. But when I saw him this time, he looked very healthy, happy, and up and out of the bed. He told me he was okay, and he loved me. After this he disappeared. It was one of the most real experiences I've ever had. It was like he was as real as you are. Is there something wrong with me? Was this a hallucination?"

"Incredible. I'm glad you shared this with me. What you encountered is called a near-death experience. People from all around the world have reported these sorts of occurrences. During this time a person dies or comes very close to physical death. After the crisis passes and once life returns, a near-death experience can be confusing for quite a while. These events are common regardless of being religious or atheist, culture, sex, gender, state of health, or socioeconomic level. So, no! There's absolutely nothing wrong with you."

"Really? I thought I was losing my mind. I even went to a psychiatrist and tried to talk to him about it. He suggested an antianxiety medication."

"Well, you need to know, I'm not the only one looking into these sorts of events. There's actually a ton of research on this topic."

"Research? Scientists researching what I had?"

"Yes! So, who else have you shared this with?"

"I told one friend of mine about it."

"What did she say?"

"She just kind of nodded at me with a sympathetic grin, while repeating several times that she really didn't know what to make of it."

"Not speaking openly about life-after-death encounters isn't only a Jewish problem but a Western civilization concern. Many people never talk to anybody else about experiences like this. If I provide you with literature about afterlife encounters, you just might relate to the words written. What about your family?"

"Oh, I don't think I want to tell my family. Not anything. They would probably make me feel crazy or tell me I need to go get stronger medication from the shrink."

"Why do you think this is? Are they religious, agnostics?"

"I know that my mom goes to synagogue occasionally. Like for the big holidays. But she's mainly there to socialize. You know, hanging out in study groups or helping with cooking. I feel like she's afraid of spirituality. She had a rough time with her father. When she was in elementary school, he became very distant and moody. His work became everything to him."

"So, would you say work was his escape?"

"Yes."

"Have your parents ever shared their history with you?"

"Not really, but I do know my mother's grandparents were in Germany during World War II. They hid out in Catholic churches. My mom talks to others whose parents were touched by the war, so maybe she could hear me out. But my dad? He's a hardcore atheist. I know a line of his family was stuck behind the Iron Curtain during the Cold War, and eventually he lost touch with them altogether. If you mention the word *god* around him, he looks like he's going to explode."

"If you were to say something to him about your experience of being raised out of your body during heart surgery and looking down on your physical self, what would he say?"

"He'd look at me like I'd lost my mind. Then he'd tell me I'm a grown woman and not a child and end with 'How can you believe in such nonsense?!' After that he'd get up in a huff and leave the room or turn on the television. With him, I'd have to tread lightly."

"If you mention this to him you might be planting a seed. He may initially be upset, but without you knowing it just might get him thinking. It could be the start of a new healing."

This reconstructed dialogue, based on conversations I've had and gathered over the last thirty years, provides a powerful example of why we should eventually share our afterlife experiences with our families. By hiding these life-changing events we are enabling family to stay stuck with unhealthy family rules, old wounds, and beliefs. One of my relatives knew about my afterlife encounters and would become distant when I'd bring them up. Imagine my surprise when I heard she was going to go listen to someone share about a near-death experience. Another cousin told me about an empathetic near-death experience he had with his ill wife. Lying sided by side, both of them felt themselves leaving their bodies and traveling through a tunnel toward a golden light. At one point my cousin's wife told him he was not allowed to go any farther. He was meant to only go so far, just far enough to catch a glimpse of where she would be after she left her earthly body behind.

SHARDS OF GLASS

When I'm a guest on a radio show, afterward I receive thought-provoking emails, texts, or messages. During these programs I share the notion that we are all part of a much greater brilliance. The listening audience then asks even more questions. Many wonder whether we retain our individuality after we cross over to the next world. At such times the following analogy can provide a teachable moment. If I were to knock over one of my favorite Depression-era green glass vases, it would shatter into hundreds of shards, each a unique shape. Though the shards remain green in color, each fragment is different and has its own "personality."

We each carry within us a distinct shard of light or piece of the source, also known as life energy. Without this, our material body would be lifeless. With near-death experiences, departing visions and after-death communication, experiencers often talk about an encounter with this greater light. With my near-death encounter, I saw a brilliant golden light leading to a bright golden tunnel. During that moment the connection was almost too much.

Serious meditators also talk about seeing a light and try to link with this source. Words and phrases used to express such encounters include *filled up, loved, not alone, one with the light, comforted, exhilarated,* and *changed forever.* This little shard of light within each of us reaches out toward an indescribable brilliance. With meditation of this nature, there are changes in how we see our fellow travelers. This shard of essence is in all things. Such an intense connection with this undefinable super consciousness not only helps us to heal but also to be of better service to others.

Recognizing physical death is not the end and that certain past rules no longer work for us helps us grow. We create a partnership with an undefinable, ever-expanding creative force. Today, I don't need to define the source of this force, but I do need to understand a shard of it, the spirit, soul, energy, or consciousness that resides within me. I'm here to cocreate with this consciousness to assist in assuring continued spiritual evolution.

THE BODY AS VESSEL FOR SOUL, FOR LIGHT

When the seven candles of the menorah (candelabra) are lit, they are said to ascend; we "raise up the candles." According to Proverbs 20:27, "the soul of man is God's candle." And another verse from Proverbs (6:23) states: "A candle is a commandment and Torah is light." Shaul Yosef Leiter, in contemplating these verses, made the following observation in an article for Chabad.org:

A candelabra has two components: the light and the vessel that holds the light. This corresponds to the soul and the body. By "raising up the candle" we not only reveal the soul in the body, but we clarify that the body is made to be a vessel for the soul.

In November of 2013, an active man who regularly played tennis met the expanded light, the Ein Sof.

Meeting the Light
David Z.

Prior to my near-death experience, I have no memory of the event. I had a sudden cardiac arrest at a tennis club on Friday, November 11, 2013. Cardiopulmonary resuscitation was given. Clinical death (cessation of breathing or heart function) occurred. This sudden cardiac arrest was caused by a 100 percent blockage of the left anterior descending artery. I woke up Tuesday, five days later, in a hospital bed. I'd been unconscious or in a "cold coma" from the event until I woke.

The experience is the only thing I remember. It was very visual, through my eyes. I was rocketed straight upward to a bright light. It was like a different galaxy or some kind of vortex in the sky. When I hit the light, everything was backward. Up became down, and I was then racing downward. As I came closer to Earth, which was in black and white, I started to see streets and houses. It felt like a town, but when I got closer, Earth then turned to blue and green in color. Upon impact, the colors expanded into an explosion of blue and green. Hugh rush. The colors were vivid. These colors brought up feelings. The impact of the color was exhilarating. Huge rush. Very fast.

The first person I told was my sister-in-law because she asked. She then told me about similar reported experiences. My encounter included an unearthly light, a light clearly of mystical or otherworldly origin. I would describe it as a solar vortex or parallel dimension. And this included a landscape or city. I felt excitement, peace, incredible pleasantness, and happiness. I felt united or one with the world.

Today, my religion is of great importance to me, but after the near-death experience, I sought out help to make sense of it all. Though I'm a conservative Jew, before the experience, I was not very active with Judaism. I know my grandfather survived the Holocaust and that he was the only survivor in his family of seven to nine members. I knew him, and he was close to my dad. He died when he was ninety years old.

It's also important to note I've been sober for nineteen years, but before the near-death experience, I was still uncertain whether an afterlife existed. Previously, I was only moderately compassionate toward others, but that's changed. I now have more compassion toward others. Today, I know an afterlife is a certainty, and I do not fear death. For me God is absolutely real, and our lives are meaningful and significant. When I revisit the experience, I still feel very emotional, but my priorities have changed. I'm looking through a whole set of different eyes, and today I celebrate two birthdays, one including my near-death experience.

David was lucky. Though no one openly discussed his grandfather's sorrowful loss during the Holocaust, David still had the history of knowing that his great-aunts, great-uncles, and others had perished. Then, when he had a near-death experience, his sister-in-law was interested and shared similar accounts. Because of this I find David to be a very blessed soul. If the previous generations of your family have not shared their secrets with you, then their feelings will be passed on down to you. Telling the stories about this history or researching one's lineage releases not only secrets but also the attached emotion.

When I discovered that my grandfather had lost his mother early in life, it became clear to me why he had such difficulty expressing open affection for my grandmother. He was young when she passed, leaving

him and his grieving father on a large ranch growing grapes. No longer having a mother in his life, any role-modeling for interacting with
women in a healthy manner essentially disappeared. Before learning
this, I thought he just wasn't very interested in me.

My grandmother, also the offspring of parents from Russia, grew up
in a village made up of only our ethnic group. She always felt inferior to
American women and wanted to pass as a member of American society.
After looking at a woman's magazine, my grandmother, a wonderful
seamstress, would whip up a modern American-style outfit, from hat
to shoes. Presenting in this manner was both about safety and wanting to blend in: "If I dress like them, I'll blend in and won't get hurt."
Regardless of her meticulous nature or diligence in sewing clothes
from pictures in fashion magazines, she constantly struggled to fit in.
Knowing this allowed me to understand why she was so strict with me,
my appearance and public behavior.

My other grandfather lost his father when he was also very young.
Then World War II ravished the family. Because of a disability, my
grandfather felt less than other men. Having this knowledge gave me
a peek into the life of shame he had endured. My grandmother on this
side of the family had a father who abandoned her and her sister for her
mother's best friend. Throughout her life she was a very harsh woman.
Never complimentary but instead typically disapproving, making any
form of closeness with her impossible.

One day I found a piece of family history that defined my
grandparents for the rest of their lives. It came in the form of a letter
from a military officer. I knew my uncle had fought as a soldier but
had no idea his passing was so tragic and violent. Shot crossing the
Rhine River, his death at twenty years of age had to be devastating
for them.

Knowing the paths my grandparents had followed allowed me to
understand many of the strong feelings I'd been carrying were about
their heartbreaking history. This knowing gave me an insight into why

they treated me the way they did. This includes not only the difficult times, but also the love they showed for me.

Having all this treasured information helped me reclaim my own spirit and evolve into the individual I was meant to be. By right-sizing my life path, my journey has become clearer and not so muddled with the pain of my ancestors.

In my clinical practice, one of the first things I want to know about the person sitting before me is what their parents and grandparents were like. Then we move on to great-grandparents and great-great-grandparents. We also pull out big sheets of paper and begin writing down the names of all the relatives in our family on a tree. You can download free genealogy trees from sites online.

After this we write underneath each name any traumas a relative may have experienced, like the Depression, Holocaust, illnesses, growing up with alcoholism, long-term unemployment, child abuse, or early death of a spouse, parent, or other relative. Family lore and rumors are also considered. Often there is truth to some of those funny stories. Yes, we start simple. Once this is accomplished, we next take out a red pen and underneath each name we write how anger, fear, depression, and grief were expressed. What did this look like? Next, we begin to examine any patterns of behavior or hurt on our tree traveling from one generation to the next.

With a blue pen we then write out how each individual reacted to pain, loss, and those around them, along with any history about religious upbringing, or lack of. What feelings did they display? Did they share hard times with family, friends, and coworkers or cover this hurt up with various coping mechanisms. What follows is a list of typical ones.

Work addiction
Silence
Raging

Suicidal, or self-destructive behavior

Overdoing for others

Feeling like the designated black sheep in the family

Perfectionism and control

Not taking care of themselves

Obsessive spending of money

Chemical dependency

Emotional distancing

Food addiction

Next, we take a blue pen and make a list of all of the qualities of our ancestors and relatives that are similar to our own. Then with a green maker we make an *X* next to those behaviors, beliefs, or actions we participate in that we don't like. After doing this, place a purple mark beside the features and assets we gratefully embrace.

Looking at our family tree, notice how emotion and behavior trickles on up from the roots of the tree, to the trunk, branches, twigs, and leaves. What does our tree look like? Were all parts of our tree nurtured and, if needed, healed? Do some sections of our tree look damaged? Are the roots solid, pulling nutrients to the smallest leaves above? Does the top greenery soak in the health of the sun and repair the rest of the tree? Like the tree, can we as a family exchange our ideas with one another, break no-talk rules, nurture, and provide and receive support while expressing our emotions freely?

This is not an exercise in placing judgment on our family. It's about reflecting on what the previous generations have been through. We embrace our past suffering, heartbreaks, and history, and then release the carried pain of the past. This is how mending starts with our generation. We must break the cycle of confusion. At the same time, we can have a greater appreciation for those who came before us.

The Tree of Life is a universal symbol found in many myths and religious traditions around the world. Among its many meanings it signifies the connection between heaven and Earth, the material world and the spiritual, body and source. With roots in the ground and branches in the sky, the initiate climbs the tree to evolve and awaken. Our tree, with its deep roots and wide trunk, may reflect parts of us, but we can still choose how our branches and leaves sprout.

EIGHT

What Is an NDE or Near-Death Experience?

Suddenly I was ejected from my body and I wasn't angry anymore. . . . I was completely that energy. . . . It was love, it was wisdom, it was dynamism.

—TIENKE KLEIN, RECOUNTING HER
NEAR-DEATH EXPERIENCE

Several years ago, I was writing a column for a publishing company. During that time, I came across information about the Holocaust few today may be aware of. There were once Jewish colonies in the Dutch East Indies, now known as Indonesia, and they were an extension of the Netherlands. These territories were under Dutch rule. In the early 1900s, Jews from Europe began to immigrate to the East Indies, and the trickle only grew. Soon colonies increased in size with new residents. With the already established Jewish community, refugees escaping the Nazis also sought safety in the Dutch East Indies.

During World War II, Nazi Germany began putting pressure on the Japanese to create an environment free of Jews. Sadly, by 1943 most if not all of Jewish society living in this part of the world found themselves interned in camps. Compared to Jews living in other colonies in Asia, this particular Jewish cluster suffered much harsher abuses and torment. The distance between the Dutch Jewish settlements and their homeland of origin in Europe was over seven thousand miles. In the 1800s an average trip by ship could take up to eight months. Four decades later I can't imagine such travel time. We would need to be "in spirit" form if we wanted to quickly travel such a distance. The Jews in Europe were trying to survive the brutality of the Nazis. Across the oceans persecuted Jewish communities found themselves trapped in death camps in the East Indies. No one was coming to rescue them.

With the Netherlands occupied by Germany, these Jewish Dutch citizens did not have the means to defend themselves from the Japanese. It was almost impossible for help of any sort to make it to the Dutch East Indies. A sad situation with no relief in sight proved to be a major trial for this community. When these colonies were occupied by the Japanese the scene was one of unspeakable terror, with sexual abuse, slavery, murders, extortion, starvation, and forced labor taking place. In comparison to European death camps, the photographs I have seen of prisoners in Japanese camps are in many respects equally gruesome.

One little girl living in the Dutch East Indies remembers her father being taken away. Just under three years of age, daughter Tienke Klein would never see this beloved man again. The grief and loss would follow her for years.

Born and raised in a Jewish family in the Netherlands, during World War II, Klein was captured by the Japanese and sent to Ambarawa prison camp in the middle of Java Island. One can only imagine what this young child was confronted with.

After surviving unthinkable terror within grim camp walls, she was finally free. Unfortunately, healing did not happen immediately or completely. Klein had a tremendous struggle recovering not only from the consequences of starvation and endless physical cruelty, but also from the surrounding daily inhumanity and carnage that had stolen her childhood. Years later, her painful history still haunted her. Feeling shackled to the past, the darkness of the Holocaust continued to follow her. It would take a bicycle accident and a near-death experience to bring her to a place where she could finally grieve the loss of her father and her imprisonment in a brutal concentration camp. For Klein, the answer wouldn't be revealed until she was in her fifties.

Like the Holocaust survivor Viktor Frankel, Klein's near-death experience would teach her that nobody can take away her freedom. In a videotaped account of her NDE, Klein said she came away with two messages: "People love as much as they are able to," and "You don't need to go anywhere." The latter, she explained, meant "I am complete. I am freedom." She realized, she said, that "ever since I came out of the prison camp, I was still trying get out of the prison camp. . . . I don't need to go anywhere to regain that freedom. . . . no one can take away the ground of the soul." The message for all of us is, regardless of our tragedies, we can still find peace and joy in life.

NEAR-DEATH EXPERIENCES FROM LONG AGO

Modern investigators are finally rediscovering what history taught us so very long ago. Traveling back to antiquity we discover there were wise elders and those experiencers who were very tuned in to the nature of an afterlife. Such experiences were nothing new. For centuries these encounters had historically been woven in to the fabric of everyday life. Life after death wasn't seen as a topic outweighing living a good life. Throughout the ages this balance has been maintained with a blueprint.

One researcher who studied a number of ancient Jewish NDEs has stated that "besides the obvious correlates of these (ancient) accounts with modern near-death experiences, it is particularly interesting that the experiencers . . . were specifically asked what they had seen during their deaths, not if they had seen anything." I believe those asking this question were wise sages and rabbis who took afterlife accounts for granted, already knowing such knowledge was a given.

The Talmud is an ancient piece of Judaic literature that documents not only Jewish law and a way to live, but also records among its pages several noteworthy otherworldly events. With the writings of the sages and rabbis, we step back in time and witness how the Torah was discussed, debated, and explored. A volume of written works based on the oral teachings of ethical decrees and declarations, the Torah has been passed on down through the generations. With patience the reader can spot at least a few afterlife encounters.

As already recounted in chapter 2, the experience of the Jewish Talmudist Rav Huna is one example of a Talmudic (oral word of God passed on down through the generations) near-death account. Though Rav Huna nearly died, he made a remarkable recovery. An analysis of this fantastic reprieve reveals to us how Rav Huna met with a super nova brilliant being teeming with infinite light and with other spiritual entities. After experiencing a review of his life, both the good and areas where he needed improvement, Rav Huna decided to go back to his body.

In addition to the Talmud and the Torah, the mystical interpretation of the Torah called the Zohar has examples of a world to come and afterlife encounters. When will we listen to our elders?

Remember Tienke Klein's NDE? She shared that when separated from her body, she too saw a brilliant light.

THE NEAR-DEATH EXPERIENCE

In 1975 Raymond A. Moody Jr., M.D., caused a major uproar within the scientific community when he published *Life After Life*. Within the pages of this book he presented numerous *near-death experiences*—a term he coined. His research was sparked by the near-death account of psychiatrist George G. Ritchie, who was clinically dead for nine minutes and reported encountering a figure he identified as Jesus Christ. Moody began finding and documenting other accounts of people who had experienced clinical death.

So, what exactly is a near-death experience and what does it generally look like? With a near-death experience, the patient is clinically dead, but when they come to, they often describe what "death" was like. Nearly all the cases I've reviewed have in common a number of eerie likenesses.

During such experiences, the patient has no heart rate, respiration, or brain wave activity. Despite this, patients share that they were conscious, aware, and watching as attempts were made to resuscitate them. Experiencers have described a sense of bursting out of their bodies and hovering near the ceiling, looking down on the scene as they were pronounced dead. When revived, they were often able to relate detailed information about what transpired while they were "dead." Repeatedly, those who have almost died come back to awareness recounting events they couldn't have possibly seen or logistically known about, such as naming a specific tool a surgeon used for surgery or reporting details of conversations in the next room. Some verbatim conversations between family and first responders are shared. Others recount in vivid details what medical procedures were used on their lifeless bodies.

Accounts of entering a tunnel and being drawn toward a light are common. In June 1997 Sharon Nachshoni, a twenty-eight-year-old father of three and an undercover soldier in the office of the Israeli prime minister, was in a horrific car accident. He was clinically dead for seventeen minutes until a stranger performed an emergency thoracostomy. In an article for My Western Wall, Rabbi Zamir Cohen quotes part of Nachshoni's story, as it appeared in an Israeli newspaper in Jerusalem on the eve of Rosh Hashanah, October 26, 2003.

After . . . he was considered dead, Sharon saw himself enter a tunnel, and was drawn after a light, until he arrived at a kind of large hall that had no end. In the hall there were many benches filled with people. All of them were happy and radiated warmth and love. All of them were dead, but they looked as complete and alive as could be.

Throughout history the subject has periodically gone underground, during which the skeptics gain a foothold in the media, but in my opinion the evidence is irrefutable. Something is happening, and we cannot just toss aside those experiencers who have had contact with the afterlife.

The NDE characteristics of today's experiencer will often involve several of the following:

The individual comes close to death or has a life-threatening experience.

At this time there can be a physical separation between the body and the soul, spirit, or consciousness.

Initial feelings of the experiencer may seem confusing but can then become pleasant and comforting.

The experiencer finds herself seeing a light, a light being, or relatives and friends who have gone before her.

Some experiencers see a tunnel of light or color.

The experiencer may not go through this tunnel or can find themselves traveling within it.

The experiencer can be greeted by light beings, deceased friends and relatives, or angels and religious divinities.

There may be an astonishing, overpowering light being at the end of the tunnel.

An extraordinary being may present as a powerful voice or music.

The experiencer can then be presented with a total review of her life in the physical world—feeling the feelings and reliving each and every moment.

The experiencer evaluates his life and learns from it.

There might be a conversation about whether or not the experiencer wants to return to the physical body.

Suddenly, the experiencer's consciousness is back in the body.

WAKING UP BEFORE I GO

A few months ago, a woman asked me if it was possible for a patient in a coma to suddenly come to after months of unconsciousness. When I told her yes, she then wanted to know if an individual in a vegetative state with a brain lacking any activity could abruptly become aware. Again, I said yes.

Why? Because not only have I witnessed this but well-known researchers have also documented the phenomena. Bruce Greyson, M.D., is professor emeritus of psychiatry and neurobehavioral sciences at the University of Virginia and has been at the head of near-death experience research for decades.* In a 2016 talk, addressing whether consciousness is produced in the brain, he had the following to say about the "suddenly awake" patient:

> There are cases published in the medical literature of patients suffering from brain abscesses, tumors, strokes, meningitis, Alzheimer's disease and other dementias, schizophrenia, and mood disorders, all of whom had long ago lost the ability to think or communicate. In many of these patients, there was evidence from brain scans, or from autopsies, that their brains had deteriorated to an irreversible degree. . . . Mental clarity returned in the last minutes, hours, or sometimes days before the patient's death.

---

*He is also the foreword writer for this book.

Greyson—or, as I call him, the "Godfather of Research into Afterlife and Near-Death Experiences"—is one of the few individuals who has influenced several generations of researchers. With great compassion and care, he has blended science and consciousness with the first-person accounts experiencers have shared with him. These include premonitions, after-death experiences, departing visions, seeing deceased relatives in dreams, or as a manifestation of how they appeared during the physical life. His latest book, *Afterlife: A Doctor Explores What Near-Death Experiences Reveal about Life and Beyond,* takes a closer look at how consciousness and brain function may be intertwined. Greyson has been doing research for a number of decades. His research recently turned another corner with an exciting, commonsense, and alternative look at death and dying. Examining the dying process as an in-between progressive transition, from one state of being to another, we see how death has a job!

Watching people on the brink of death, having had no consciousness or brain activity for months, suddenly rally and start engaging in conversation with everybody in the room is an awe-inspiring experience. Once awake they appear happy, at peace, and interested in family, other relatives, hospital workers, nurses, and doctors who come to visit them. This is indeed a curious phenomenon. Like the deathbed or departing vision, patients also seem to know where they will be going after death. Several have told me they have already seen where they will be once they leave their physical bodies.

In spite of having a brain that is incredibly damaged, they still know all the people in the room or at the bedside by name and then will coherently discuss past or upcoming events. It's as if they've received a message from somewhere while comatose. Consciousness has separated from the body and already investigated a world to come. By choice or some other unknown reason, once awake a message is shared. More research into this aspect of such afterlife experiences needs to be done. That said, what do these anecdotal incidences say about the nature of consciousness? While scratching our heads, this does give us something to think about. The story below of Dan Brodsky-Chenfeld—a champion skydiver who survived a plane crash in 1992 that killed sixteen people—also forces us to scratch our heads.

Surviving a Deadly Fall from High Altitude
Dan Brodsky-Chenfeld

In spring 1992, I was in a plane crash. The plane was carrying skydivers. Sixteen out of twenty-two people on board were killed at the crash. I have no memory of it and was in a coma for over a month. When I woke from the coma, I had no idea where I was or what had happened. But there was one crystal-clear memory in my head.

It wasn't a dream. It was as real as any real-world experience I had ever had. I could remember the entire thing, every action, every word, and every thought. It went like this: I was in free fall. Almost as if I had just appeared there. I love free fall and finding myself there at that moment seemed natural. I was at home, at peace, part of the infinite sky. But after a few seconds I noticed that this wasn't normal free fall. It was quieter. The wind wasn't blowing as fast. I wasn't descending. A gentle breeze was suspending me. It was okay; it was fine. I was floating, flying, but it wasn't right. What was I doing there? I wasn't afraid. I felt safe but confused. I looked up and saw James flying down to me just as if we were on a skydive together, and he was swooping me. His expression was that silly, playful smile he so often had in free fall. He obviously was not confused at all. He knew exactly where he was and what he was doing there.

He flew down and stopped in front of me. Still with a smile on his face, he asked, "Danny, what are you doing here?" I answered, "I don't know." James said, "You're not supposed to be here. You have to get back down there." I began to get a grasp of the situation. I asked him, "Are you coming with me?" His expression changed to one with a hint of sadness. He said, "No, I can't." I tried to persuade him to change his mind, "C'mon, James, we were just getting started. You gotta come with me."

James raised his voice, interrupting me. "I can't!" It was obvious that the decision was final. It seemed as if it wasn't his decision. He continued with a gentle smile. "I can't, but it's okay. There are more places to go, more things to do, more fun to have. Tell my mom it's okay. Tell her I'm okay."

For a few seconds we just looked at each other as I accepted this for the reality it was. He changed his tone and spoke with some authority as he gave me an order. "Now," he said, "you need to get back down there. You need to go get control of the situation."

Brodsky-Chenfeld shared with me one of the most incredible near-death experiences I've reviewed in over 30 years. Though he survived this tragic crash he was still left in terrible shape. After six weeks in a coma, Brodsky-Chenfeld finally came to, only to discover that, along with serious internal injuries, he'd suffered from a collapsed lung, a broken neck, severe head trauma, and a broken skull. During his coma he found himself very aware but noted he'd lost a sense of his body. For him the experience was "entirely pleasant." Brodsky-Chenfeld added that though he did feel confusion and sadness, he also felt comfort, at peace, and happy. Physically alert just before his collision with the ground below and while medically unconscious after the accident, he could see and hear everything that happened during his NDE.

This award-winning international sky diver, teacher, and author also had an encounter with his best friend, James, who had perished in this catastrophe. James, who was like a little brother to him, actually spoke to him and told Dan he couldn't be with him; it wasn't Dan's time to go and he had to go back. He also asked Dan to pass on a message to his mother, telling her he was all right. To this day Brodsky-Chenfeld says the memory of what he saw and experienced while separated from his body continues to be very strong.

During my NDE, I remember feeling very at one with everything around me, the universe, galaxy, and infinity. This is a common sensation for most experiencers. Brodsky-Chenfeld said he experienced an intense nonnegotiable understanding that he was united and connected with infinity.

For those who encounter such an experience the fear of physical death dissipates. Though Jewish, Brodsky-Chenfeld shared he was only somewhat involved with this religion, and he still had fears about death. After his otherworldly encounter, he no longer felt frightened of death. In reviewing Brodsky-Chenfeld's event, his brush with physical death, I began to see that his experience had been a spiritual awakening. He moved from a hopeful belief to one that gave him true assurances that the demise of physical life wasn't the end of life. Ideas that Brodsky-Chenfeld had about life after death were confirmed as true, and he now believes there is some sort of god or force that truly exists.

Dan Brodsky-Chenfeld had a powerful experience that left him knowing there is purpose to this life and that the material world was just part of a very long journey. His friend James had come to him. This proved to Dan love is real.

LETTERS OF ADMIRATION

As I said earlier, I found Dan's experience to be not only of spiritual significance but also of extreme value to the rest of us. Below are a few of the communications I shared with him.

Dear Dan,

When we have such an experience these events imprint upon our soul.

Regular, everyday dreams usually have to do with releasing any stress we've experienced throughout the day. Most of the time we don't even remember these dreams. Then there are those dreams which are about trauma. This is when we revisit our trauma of origin and go through all of the difficult times during that ordeal.

What you experienced was very different. You were introduced to a doorway into another dimension of reality. It is within this reality that those who have gone before us can reach out and make contact. You received a message from your friend who had already departed, letting you know you were going to be all right. But he also added that you needed to get "back down there" (the earth plane), and sort this out. It's a type of after-death communication. Loved ones who have made the trip to the next phase of our evolution can come to us to leave us with a message.

Before it was popular or there was much interest, I'd been researching departing visions for decades. And I've collected over two thousand accounts. Plus, I've had a few experiences like this myself. I don't need to tell you your experience with your dear friend was something very, very, special. You two connected, with him moving on and you returning to the physical.

Know that your friend is around you. He hasn't left you.

In light,
Carla

This remarkable account is difficult to debate. As Dan said the experience remains crystal clear in his mind, and he can go back to this particular memory without any difficulty. If you really ponder his account, you will realize what a miracle he is. First of all, look at what he survived. Next, examine his encounter with his deceased friend. Dan's friend came to him to let him know he would make it, and then emphasized he must survive because he still had things to do on the earth plane.

As a wonderful author and powerful motivational speaker, Dan has been able to show thousands of people around the world that we do have purpose to our lives. One might think this is the end of his fantastic story, but what he learned from his afterlife journey continues to unfold. My final communication with Dan was as follows:

Hi Dan,

Thank you so much for responding to my email. Your story is incredible. There are numerous facets to it. First of all, I wanted to validate that what you encountered with your beloved friend was a true near-death experience and after-death departing vision with a message. James was definitely there. Consciousness leaves the body when we are near death. As you have discovered, during these moments we are often greeted by those who have gone before us. I had a near-death experience during a hospital stay. Such events can change our lives.

I can't imagine how hard it was for you to lose such a dear friend, along with other close colleagues who physically perished. Your injuries, along with your long hospital stay, sound incredibly painful and grueling. My heart goes out to you. What you have done with your life since this is a testament to your healing. You have helped many.

Again, thank you so much for allowing me to share your story.

Carla

Being Jewish had no influence on what Dan experienced. If anything, the event cleared up spiritual questions he'd been wrestling with. Aside from the fact that Dan is a very engaging, inspiring miracle of miracles, he brings much hope to those seekers he lectures to. I was fighting breast cancer when I put together his story. Feeling undone with emotion, his account gave me the motivation and courage to carry on. Dan continues to skydive to this today. If I had the opportunity, I'd definitely want to take a lesson or two from him.

Releasing Fear-Induced Thinking

Too many people in the public arena continue to insist that only certain religions can talk about afterlife encounters. For the most part Jews are not included in the conversation. This insinuation is far from reality. As we have seen in this and previous chapters we don't need to practice a certain philosophy or religion to find ourselves speaking with those who have already preceded us to the next world.

Years ago, I had a guest in my home who became very angry with me when I began talking about afterlife events. His religious beliefs were a bit different from mine, which at the beginning of the conversation was not a problem. He then asked me what I did for a living, and my response was clinical trauma, dying, death, and assisting in healing the families afterward. When I told him about the deathbed visions I'd witnessed at the bedside of so many, he became irate, as if I'd just slugged him in the face.

He told me, "That couldn't have happened to you because you're a woman. And secondly, you don't believe in what is right or practice the expected traditions in order to be in a position to say such things." Here he was sitting at my dining room table, eating the food I had cooked, while telling me that not only were my experiences erroneous, but because I was a woman, I shouldn't even be speaking, let alone investigating, whether or not there was an afterlife. Was I initially shocked and offended? Yes. At first, I felt very shamed, degraded, and humiliated. Was this man going to silence me? Absolutely not.

Many of us are ruled by fear. We then layer anger or extreme self-righteousness on top of the fear to give us a false sense of distance and protection from this emotion. This is also an unconscious reaction. In reality we are afraid of the unknown. We can't predict, control, or understand what is unfamiliar to us. And what can be more unknown than death? We don't want to talk about it with anybody and be seen as weak or stupid. This may work for a while, but the downside is, if we can't walk through our fear it will only grow larger.

This fear-induced way of thinking can keep us from discovering our true authentic selves. Just imagine what it would be like if we didn't allow ourselves to get wrapped in fear. What creativity would spring from our souls? How would we use the time previously dedicated to fear to now help humanity? Can you imagine such a world?

If the consequence to reducing fear is so positive, why do so many of us respond with extreme skepticism before we have examined all the collected data? Sadly, the door is shut, not letting in one photon of light. Our assumptions are then based only on inaccurate data or slanted research. The obsession that says life after death is a myth is just a distraction or barrier to other belief systems, considerations, and opportunities. By accepting the prospect that we don't die after physical death, we might then need to ask,

Am I evolving into the authentic person I've always wanted to be?

What have I missed out on?

Has my fear allowed me to avoid taking risks?

Why do I feel so unfulfilled?

Are there things I've wanted to do but have been too frightened to explore?

Have I looked at my relationships that are not resolved or healed?

To be true to myself have I looked at the passing of those I love, divorces, medical hardships, the jobs I hate?

Are there mistakes I've made, and adventures I've given up for the
false safety of rudimentary tasks and beliefs?

Do I find I might need to find the courage to muster up the strength
to revisit these unsettled concerns?

Just food for thought. Truth be told I've rarely come across an
experiencer who walked away from an afterlife event not feeling clearer
and more optimistic with his or her own evolving life path. Feeling an
increased sense of adventure about the world around us, while embracing emotions full force, we are ready to take some sort of action. With
this thought in mind, I'm going to share a story.

LETTING GO OF THE BOOGEYMAN AND THE GOLEM

Many of us at any early age, say under the age of five, believed the boogeyman was real. This imaginary creature who hid at the back the closet or
under the bed was out to get us, scare us, and even hurt us. As frightened
as we might have been, the boogeyman provided an important mental
health service. This invented illusion was a way for youngsters to dis-
charge anxiety, and it worked. Hiding ourselves away under bed covers
hoping the boogeyman would not come our way helped many of us to
release any pent-up emotion we'd collected during the day.

We didn't know what the boogeyman looked like, so we used our
childlike minds and imaginations to create a visualization of this dark
monster. Along with this we would construct a personality for such a
character. When things went wrong in our little world, we could then
blame it on the boogeyman. This powerful childhood distraction could
reduce the everyday fears of a young life.

As we grew older, we discovered the boogeyman wasn't quite so
scary and maybe not even real. So, we started taking risks by poking
our head into the dark recesses of the closet and were surprised no one

was there. With more practice and exploration, we found ourselves stepping into the closet and looking under the bed. With practice grew confidence. Eventually, our entire bedroom, including all its dark places, became a sanctuary. Because the boogeyman was no longer needed, letting go was not hard to do.

In Judaism there is a well-known folk tale about a creature first made with clay and then magically infused with life. He was called *Golem,* which means "undeveloped" or "incomplete." Because the Jews had been persecuted throughout the ages, there was an essential need for protection, and a rabbi was said to have created the Golem as a caretaker and protector. At first the defending Golem served a positive role by reducing the fear of Jewish persecution. Like the boogeyman, the Golem had a job to do. For a while this worked.

The power to survive is incredibly strong, and the more attached we become to an idea, the more power we give it. It's like being in a safe cozy space, believing we are hidden from the harshness of life. By wrapping our souls in beautiful illusionary blankets, this idea serves a purpose and works well for a while. Then we get curious about the outside world. We want to explore it, but it's scary. In the story of the Golem, we see the beast becomes consumed with power and won't let go. Being needed gave him purpose, but now he is lost, no longer a safe caretaker.

Eventually, the Golem crumbles or explodes. What was once seen as a guardian and friend now becomes terrifying and frightening. Thinking we need to give the decaying Golem more power to heal, we give more of ourselves so that he will be there for us. Because of fear we can lose ourselves within the shadows of the once mighty Golem. Sadly, the creature begins to self-destruct. We think we need to escape into the arms of a protector because we don't like seeing our clay guardian disintegrate to the ground. Thankfully, there is a solution. With work, we finally break free from the fear of the unknown and we let go of the Golem.

If we Jews go public with our afterlife experiences, we are not betraying our religion. Nor do we have to give up our own philosophy about life. We will not become crazy people who sit around cross-legged all day dressed in flower-print tops and smoking some plant. Ridicule will only go as far as we let it. Allowing ourselves to take risks and begin to explore isn't always comfortable. There are no boxes or hidden rooms to escape to. Instead, we become explorers of the unknown. Not having concrete answers no longer impacts the way we look at possibilities. Moving through a few difficult days and many good days, eventually we discover we can think for ourselves and ask those questions we've always wanted to ask. This is how we deflate fear.

Once on our path we realize the journey never ends. Instead of running away from different ideas, we cautiously seek to learn. There is no need to accept everything. We take away what feels right and leave the rest. Remember, this is our time of exploration. There is no need to be polite by accepting what has been stuffed down our throats. We trust those who have provided us with wonderful, thought-provoking ideas, while allowing ourselves to be our own best investigators.

Remember this journey is for you. It is your time. You too can banish both the boogeyman and the Golem, replacing them with the wonder of what's out there. Knowing there is so much to explore, you are ready for the challenge. It is yours. Take the risk.

NINE

Reincarnation in Judaism

The usual Hebrew term for reincarnation is gilgul, "rolling," that
is, the soul "rolls" through time from one body to a different body.
— RABBI LOUIS JACOBS,
THE JEWISH RELIGION: A COMPANION

Those outside of Judaism often throw all of Judaism into one giant pot. Some Jews are religious while others are just culturally Jewish, only sticking to the traditions they grew up with. Other Jews are secular, not heavily involved with either religion or culture. Along with this are the different sects of Judaism: Hasidic, Orthodox, Modern Orthodoxy, Reform, Reconstructionist, Humanistic Movement, and more. Each sect has its own opinion about reincarnation, and today, they continue to disagree with one another.

Thinkers and rabbis from most sects of Judaism have attempted to lay out all ideas regarding reincarnation. According to a Yeshshem article ("Basic Class 11—Reincarnation"), a number of rabbis believed in reincarnation, among them Nachmanides, Rabbenu Bahya ben Asher, Levi ibn Habib, and Isaac ben Solomon Luria. Isaac Luria (1534–1572) was a leading rabbi and Jewish mystic in the Galilee region of Ottoman Syria, now Israel. The article notes that:

Isaac Luria taught new explanations of the process of gilgul, and identification of the reincarnations of historic Jewish figures, which were compiled by Hayyim ben Joseph Vital in his Shaar HaGilgulim. The idea of gilgul became popular in Jewish folk belief, and is found in much Yiddish literature among Ashkenazi Jews.

According to ancient and modern Jewish literacy, along with oral tradition, when physical death occurs, the essence of our being can move into a different physical identity to begin a new adventure. This idea isn't unknown to most rabbis. The internationally known author and respected rabbi Pinchas Winston wrote in his book *The Fundamentals of Reincarnation*:

> The Hebrew term for "reincarnation" is *"gilgul,"* like the word *"galgal,"* which means "wheel." A soul in a body can go from birth to death, and to birth again, through a cycle involving reincarnation. Reincarnation allows a person to accomplish a degree of rectification in his next life which he failed to achieve in his previous one. If one dies before reaching his highest level of soul possible, he can continuously reincarnate to complete his *tikkun* until he succeeds.

For years any concept of reincarnation was confusing for me. None of the rabbis or clergy I talked with ever explained reincarnation in a way that made any sense; many blew it off to old superstitions. Thinking back to childhood years, I don't ever remember talking to my Hebrew teacher, rabbi, cantor, or youth adviser about the recycling of the souls or *gilgul*.

As I got older, I began to see metaphors in different Judaic ancient literature discussing the wheel of life and how life of some sort continues to go on after physical death. I started looking into ancient literature along with stories from modern-day afterlife or reincarnation experiencers from a long time ago. Right there in front of me, I found bits and pieces of discussion about reincarnation tucked into the backdrop of Judaic history. Exploring modern-day experiences and debate hinting toward ideas of reincarnation, I wondered why this topic was such a big secret. After years of study, I finally found a concept or philosophy about reincarnation that worked for me. I'd already had a few experiences with reincarnation and moved away from the fluffy New Age to start exploring what was already in my religion. With study, I became even more curious about my own encounters. Such exploration led me on a journey that would help me better understand myself and aid in my spiritual evolution. What follows are fairly modern-day reincarnation experiences.

THE SPARK OF LIFE WE ALL SHARE

I'm a unique physical being: my physical body wasn't ripped off some rack of cookie-cutter dresses. But once the earth coat turns to dust, will I just be a soul among souls? How will I be able to continue to rectify all my remaining concerns, unfinished business, and resentments or achieve my full potential? As I continued to investigate, I just became more confused. A little common sense would be needed to start sorting all of this out.

Our likes and dislikes can be similar but are still not the same. Even identical twins aren't replicas of one another. Identical twins can have different fingerprints. One can be left-handed while the other is a right-hander. From person to person, our sense of smell can be different. If a house is burning anywhere on Galveston Island, I'll smell it immediately. At the same time my husband will look around and ask, "What?"

Despite these divergent characteristics, underneath our corporeal dress we all carry the exact same life energy. Me, along with my dog, cat, bird, and turtle, all need this spiritual "oomph" to function. If this is true, does this come from one higher source or something beyond our comprehension? How does this spark affect us on a more spiritual level?

In my book *One Last Hug before I Go*, I wrote of an experience a rabbi shared with me about his son. The very young toddler was looking at photographs he had never seen. One picture really caught his eye. Turning to his father, the rabbi, the boy announced, "I know the people in the picture." He added he was with them before he came "here." The rabbi looked at the images and quickly realized the people his son recognized were the rabbi's parents who had passed before his son was born. The spark of life communicates from one generation to the next.

We all share this spark of life. When I was a kid living among the grapevines of California, I was surprised when my teacher said that energy could not be destroyed. This was extremely baffling, and so for several years I became fixated on figuring out the riddle. Today, I believe we all hold deep within us a shard of otherworldly essence. Though the physical body eventually turns to dirt, this glimmer of brilliance cannot be destroyed.

THE KNIGHTS TEMPLAR AND THE JEWISH ELDERS

With the birth of my sons, I made a commitment to take them traveling with me when I went to do lectures or workshops outside the United States. Both Michael and I wanted to give our boys a broader sense of the world. In doing this they learned there was more to life than fast food and video games. After a stay in Wales, my oldest son even started asking for starters instead of appetizers.

One year I was asked to provide a workshop for a treatment center in England. Before our plane had even landed, I'd begun to feel extremely agitated. Something just didn't feel right, and I'm a seasoned traveler.

When venturing outside the states we would make our own accommodations months before a trip. For some dumb reason this time we didn't do so. Jetlagged and hungry we discovered only one room had been provided for us at a hotel. This is not an uncommon situation. Previously we had always found a way to make it work. With this trip the situation was ridiculous. The room was the size of a small closet.

After sighing and listening to the whining of my children, fast thinking was a must. Thankfully, there were several fancy pillows on a chair, and my husband was able to rustle up some blankets. We made one little pallet on the floor next to the only small bed in the room. Michael then pushed two chairs together. He slept under the chairs while my youngest snored loudly on the top, surrounded by bathroom towels and rolls of unopened toilet paper. Dinner consisted of goldfish, jelly fruit worms, and an apple. Our situation could have been so much worse. Just ask me about communist Belarus.

The next morning, we packed up all our gear and went down to the lobby to wait for somebody from the treatment center to pick us up. The lesson was, watch those expectations. No one arrived. With this Michael pulled out our fold-up stroller. I removed my heels and put on a pair of flats. Grabbing our oldest son's hands, Michael began making his way to a tube station while I pushed our youngest in the stroller. We arrived at our destination sweating and dirty. Regardless of our misadventure, the workshop was a success.

For the next lecture Michael had already planned for accommodations, so the boys were able to sleep on pull-out trundle beds. There was also an inexpensive family eatery next door. It was heaven. The next morning, we did some sightseeing. The boys love castles, swords, axes, knives, shields, and knight's armor, so life was good!

Before we returned to our hotel, I had a sudden, weird urge to see a Knights Templar round church. I knew there was one in London, so off to the races we went. For me the search for the church started to feel overwhelmingly necessary. I found my emotions were extremely confusing, and my husband thought I'd lost my mind. After ice cream cones and a ride to the Templar tube station we found ourselves next to the Thames River. Michael's job was to keep the boys out of the river while I went looking for a round building. Eventually, we found it.

The structure was like nothing I'd ever seen before. Regardless, it felt very familiar. While I was frantically knocking on the door to see if anyone would let me in, the boys were now running around the building. Finally, a caretaker of the sanctuary came along. By this time, I was unhinged. In spite of my emotional state, he let me into the building. I was grateful but still didn't understand what was happening. Pacing across beautiful floors, my emotions, sadness, fear, and grief were beginning to become uncontainable. The mad woman inside was about to surface.

Within the sanctuary, a group of age-old effigies were laid out on a stone floor. There was one statue to which I was especially drawn. Moving closer, my feelings churned. Tears were welling up in my eyes. At that time, I had no idea who this particularly worn effigy represented. Decades ago, there were no barriers separating the public from the statues. Names or labeling on these figures were not there. Regardless, I was somehow intertwined with this one effigy.

Leaving the temple, this powerful experience had to be buried into the very deep recesses of my mind. With the help of some greasy fish and chips, it took me several hours to settle down. The experience with the round church had been so intense that to regain any sense of stability I had to put it aside.

Because there were no labels or name plates on the effigies, I decided to investigate and accidently discovered the effigy was that of a well-known Templar knight. He had given up titles, luxury, and lands for poverty and the life of a religious soldier. He and eight other knights who had been born into or were somehow related to houses of royalty had banded together. They then laid down the foundation for the Templar order. Fighting military knights along with those who didn't join in battle grew to twenty thousand persons. In a 2021 article ("The Origin of the Knights Templar—Descendants of Jewish Elders?"), researcher Mark Amaru Pinkham observes that "according to the modern Templar historians, Tim Wallace-Murphy and Christopher Knight, the knights who banded together as the Knights Templar were part of a wave of European royalty descended from Jewish Elders that had fled the Holy Land around 70 AD, when it was invaded by the Romans." All Templar treasures, including scrolls, were hidden from invading Romans at secret sites. By doing this the hope was the Romans would not have an opportunity to loot this religious history, including precious documents related to Jewish law, philosophy, and mysticism. After escaping the Middle East, these Jewish Elders made their way to Europe and married into royal families. According to Pinkham when trauma and war began in the Holy lands, many descendants of the original Elders living in Europe and the Middle East took up shields and swords to protect the persecuted.

Blessed in 1185 by Heraclius, patriarch of Jerusalem, the order of Templar, also known as the order of Solomon's Templar, was founded after the first crusade at the site of King Solomon's Temple in Jerusalem. Though Hollywood has presented the Templars as a marauding band slaughtering people, left and right, they protected Christians and Jews, along with other pilgrims traveling to and from the Holy Lands.

Before the First Crusade, there are stories of compatible business and financial relationships between Christians and Jews. Though the two groups were culturally different, they still associated with one another, even attending each other's social gatherings, like a nuptial or ritual for a physical passing. During that period in history, what could these groups have learned from each other? What were their conversations like?

At the beginning of the rise of the Knights Templar there were prophecies about millenniums to come. Like other investigators I've discovered numerous ancient religious groups who embraced some form of philosophy about the continuous circle of life. Reincarnation was part of Christian teachings until 553 CE, when Emperor Justinian I had the teachings banned by a synod. Ancient and contemporary groups who believed in the reincarnation include the Kabbalists, Cathars, Druze, Knights Templar, Freemasons, and Rosicrucians.

In my humble opinion several disagreements about reincarnation have been ping-ponging back and forth for centuries. According to Yerachmiel Tilles in his article "Judaism and Reincarnation": "the holy Ari explained it most simply: every Jew must fulfill all 613 mitzvot, and if he doesn't succeed in one lifetime, he comes back again and again until he finishes." The Holy Ari (1534–1572), also known as Rabbi Yitzchak Luria, was one of the most famous rabbis and very religious. Every day he performed a ritual dip in the *mikvah* or purification bath. Nearing death, he instructed his followers to bathe his body in a mikvah after he died. According to legend, while the rabbi's body was being dressed for burial, he rose and put himself in the mikvah.

Embedded below the London Templar church, near a vault deep below stone effigies, are the remains of a number of knights. The politics of the Middle Ages and greed created the perfect storm for the persecution of the Templars. As times grew worse a group of this order escaped to Scotland. Their graves can be seen on the grounds of Rosslyn Chapel and Cemetery. I went down into the crypt of this Scottish sanctuary way before Hollywood picked up on this history. Here, I saw the graves of these knights. The artifacts and antiquity I touched were not like those depicted in high-drama blockbuster movies.

BACK TO SCOTLAND

The above discussion shows us that reincarnation was taken for granted by most ancient religions. Fast-forward to today the next question: Have you ever felt you've lived a previous life? Wondered if you have existed before? Felt very connected to a certain place, city, parts of the world, certain types of foods, or written works? Or have talents or natural abilities you can't explain away? I want to share a personal experience I had about a decade ago in Scotland.

We had driven from England to Scotland. And I must say this journey was very scary. Michael kept getting lost in little villages and making the local people extremely angry with his driving. Grandmothers were giving him the "up yours" (it doesn't look like a peace sign) as we traveled on narrow cobbled roads. Chauffeuring the family while driving on the left side of the road wasn't exactly his cup of tea.

Before this trip I'd already had an incredibly strong need to return to Scotland. It was so powerful. After twisting and turning over mountains and hills full of purple heather, I felt like I was returning to a place I'd known before.

As we slowly started dragging our grouchy boys up the mountainous hill, we saw a very odd-looking castle. My sons had learned about old fortresses, so they were thrilled to see more of the real thing. So, off they went, racing up the hill and raising havoc in the first part of the castle. I heard my husband yelling, "No! You cannot touch that!" Needing space, I turned the other way toward the outdoors for a much-needed breath of fresh air.

Walking outside I saw another ancient-looking building. After making my way through a sort of cavelike opening, I found myself inside a stone prison. A chill forced me to zip up my jacket. There was something about the place that scared me to death. The longer I stayed the more anxious I became. An urge to bolt out of the small prison was about to become a reality.

Standing in the middle of the room, I thought, "Who had suffered here so terribly?" Then I caught an image of a man, shackled to the left side of the prison wall, screaming in agony. The tortured soul I sensed, saw, and heard had a medium reddish-brown head of hair. His hands were locked in clamps attached to the wall of the prison, and he was terrified. Dressed well, he also felt very connected to the castle. Briefly, I had a strong sense that I was supposed to know this sobbing, distressed person.

When it comes to such incidents, I've never felt rattled, but with this I knew I couldn't stay any longer. Running out of the jail, I found I was short of breath.

When I finally felt grounded, I started making my way around the outside of this estate. Eventually, I reached the other side of the small prison. On the right front entryway, I found a description of the castle. There was also a small picture of a man. As I looked at this image, I knew this was the man I had seen chained in the prison. Then I read on the marker that this individual had been sent to this prison, but there were no words as to why. Had I lived or worked in this castle once before?

Not long after our trip to Scotland, I had what is called a medical reading. Here a sensitive can check problem areas in the body clairvoyantly. Struggling with a chronic disease that continued to pop up, I wanted a solution, and thankfully I received one. After listening to the reading, the sensitive ended by saying, "Are you aware that in a previous life you were a Scottish soldier who returned home from a battle to lots of children?"

PAST LIVES AS HOLOCAUST SURVIVORS

In an article for Aish.com, Sara Yoheved Rigler recounted the childhood experiences of a woman, Jackie Warshall, born in 1950 to American-born parents, who inexplicably had vivid memories of the Holocaust.

> When she was four years old, at night after her mother tucked her in and left her to go to sleep, little Jackie would stare into her pillow as if it were a TV set, and see a vision. She saw herself inside the back of a truck filled with women. Some of them were collapsing to the floor. Then she saw herself fly out of the truck. There, above the

truck, she would feel a sense of liberation, and say, "I got out. I'm free now."

Decades later Jackie learned that the Nazis' first experiment in mass murder was to crowd frightened people into the back of a truck and pipe carbon monoxide gas into the back of the vehicle. This little girl hadn't had any contact with the Holocaust. Recurring fearful nightmares about Nazis, carbon monoxide gas, and women collapsing to the floor in a truck would be very upsetting to a girl of four.

In 1991 Bruce Whittier, a Canadian farmer living in Nova Scotia, not only dreamt about being a Holocaust victim hiding with his family but also of a specific time piece and where it could be found. The following account comes from a 2013 article in Listverse by Sabine Bevers, which documented ten cases of supposed reincarnation:

> His name had been Stefan Horowitz, a Dutch Jew who was discovered in his hiding place along with his family and taken to Auschwitz, where he died. During and after the dreams, [Whittier] felt panicked and restless. He began to record his dreams, and one night he dreamed about a clock, which he was able to draw in detail upon waking.

Whittier decided to go looking for the old-world device and successfully found it along with its history, which convinced him that he really had led a past life. How could this man have known who he had been in a former life and what his name from his past life was? How could he know that in his former life he'd died during the Holocaust and see in his dreams a particular clock belonging to his past life? Finally, how could he discover from the shop keeper that the clock had been sold to the shop by a retired German major in the Netherlands?

There are numerous reports from those who believe they were Holocaust survivors in a past life. Many of them have had little if any contact with Judaism. For some, recall begins in childhood, while for others such memories surface decades later.

One friend of mine, who I knew to be a caring, funny, grounded pillar of the community, grabbed me after a function. Clinging to me, the poor woman was shaking from head to toe. I'd never seen her this upset. I can personally vouch for her sobriety and responsible nature, so her level of fear frightened me. To my knowledge I'd never heard one word about the Holocaust from her. As we stood outside the room where the gathering had taken place, she began talking to me about being a Holocaust victim in a past life. Speaking about visions of brutal death in her dreams, she said she had once been an extremely thin and unhealthy person.

Since that time, I've listened to several accounts like this, both in and out of my clinical practice. Discussions of camps, stripped clothing, lice, murder, crowded trains, and other Holocaust scenarios can come from all walks of life. These individuals with vivid past-life memories of the Holocaust suffer trauma symptoms much like those of Holocaust survivors.

Why would people in other countries practicing different religions have visions or memories about being Holocaust survivors? And how are these recollections so accurate? The skeptics always come up with some sort of excuse. After reviewing a number of these, consistency from one account to another is something to look at.

K. M. Wehrstein in her article about these memories ("Past Life Memories of the Holocaust") recorded the story of David Llewelyn, an English boy born in 1970. As a child, David suffered from nightmares featuring black pits full of bodies and people with guns. In early childhood, he was unable to sleep in small rooms.

[He] compulsively kept the door open and window-curtains closed. When he began writing he wrote from right to left. When he drew, he always included a star, though at the same time he had a phobia of stars, particularly the Star of David. Once he fled a shop after seeing a Star of David necklace. He had a marked fear of camps; when his mother suggested a family vacation at a camp, he said, "No. There is no happiness there. People are caged in and cold, hungry, and frightened. They'll never get out."

He told his mother the people were skeletal-looking, bald, and frightened, wearing stripped clothing. David also appeared to understand kashering and asked his mother if all the blood had been taken out of the meat she was serving. Kashering meat involves a detailed process; the meat requires processing using very strict methods. I remember my grandmother kashering meat by drawing the blood out of it. It was strange that this young boy, who wasn't Jewish, knew about this.

Although the term *Holocaust* generally refers to the systematic mass murder of the Jewish people in German-occupied Europe, the Nazis also persecuted and murdered a large number of non-Jewish people who were also considered subhuman (*Untermenschen*) or undesirable. Among those killed were approximately 250,000 German citizens with mental and physical disabilities, who the Nazis deemed a burden on society. Also exterminated were Jehovah's Witnesses, Muslims, the Roma, Poles, captured Soviet soldiers, homosexuals, and people considered to be asocial. Considering the millions who suffered so tragically, is it a stretch to see how these victims could also reincarnate?

ANCIENT WORDS

At age three, my youngest son, Josh, had a wonderful encounter with a friend from the afterlife. As recounted previously in chapter 3, he began speaking an Aramaic word, *damus,* he never could have known. According to Josh, Damus was a good guy who had come to take my dying father-in-law to the "sky." Later, I learned from a rabbi that this Aramaic word meant "angel of death." Josh talked about this angel for one full week before his grandfather passed over. Most modern-day Jews have no awareness of the Aramaic language.

What do you make of this? Just a fluke? I discovered I wasn't the only mother of a child who spontaneously spoke Aramaic. I picked up *Soul Searching,* a book written by afterlife researcher Rabbi Yaakov Astor. Within the work were quotes from well-known psychiatrist, author, and past-life researcher Dr. Brian Weiss. Flipping through the pages I saw two words that caught my attention, *reincarnation* and *Aramaic.* I read with great interest Weiss's account of a case in which the parents of two-year-old twin boys brought them to the Linguistics Department at Columbia University because the boys were speaking a sophisticated private language. The department determined they were speaking Aramaic, a language still spoken in a few remote villages in Syria. The questions were: How did they know this? Where was this coming from? How can this be explained?

THE CATERPILLAR AND THE MOTH: NATURE'S PROOF OF REINCARNATION

I know I overthink everything, so I will try to not complicate the cornflakes. Here is an incredibly simplistic analogy for reincarnation. Over our current lifetime we evolve and change physically. During this same time, we learn lessons that help us fine-tune our spirit. Change happens but the essential light of us remains. When we shed this body, our true being gears up for the next evolution. Nature can teach us a great deal. For example, the many lives of the caterpillar can give us something to think about.

One afternoon I was watering my tomato plants when I saw a beautiful green caterpillar. I watched him crawl from leaf to leaf, eating up my pretty little potted friends. This caterpillar, a tomato hornworm, is bound to become a five-spotted hawk moth. I wondered: Are caterpillars the only ones who change from one form to another? If I were like the caterpillar, would I one day dispose of my cocoon to experience new knowledge? Would I physically find myself embodied in another form of beauty? Am I like the moth?

The insect on my tomato bush experiences and learns all about being a caterpillar. During this time the creature will shed its skin five times, growing bigger each time. Though looking a bit different with each change, its essence is still that of its species: *Manduca quinquemaculata*.

As the creature changes in size and even appearance, its inner motivation to ravage my garden remains. Here we have the inner soul of the caterpillar form of *M. quinquemaculata*. After living for a certain length of time as a caterpillar, the challenging work for this span of time is complete; the job is done. Now, another big change is about to occur. After building and then sleeping in a cozy cocoon, the insect eventually emerges from its rest with beautiful wings and a need for different nourishment. With different mouth parts, it is unable to eat leaves, and nectar from flowers becomes the food of choice.

Though this insect radically changes its shape, it remains the same species. It has gone from tomato hornworm to five-spotted hawk moth but has remained throughout *M. quinquemaculata*. Along with graceful wings, different coloring, and diet, it continues to retain the soul of its species. This is how nature reincarnates.

What about us? Do we reincarnate? Over our lifetime we evolve and change physically, while fine-tuning our spirit. Change happens, but our inner light remains the same. When we shed this body suit, our true being gets ready for the next level of advancement. Never complicate the cornflakes. It's obvious.

DECIDING TO RETURN

The air is full of souls; those who are nearest to earth descending to be tied to mortal bodies, return to other bodies, desiring to live in them.

—PHILO JUDAEUS, *DE SOMNIIS* (1:22)

As we've seen we have been jumping on and off the wheel of life for several millennium. In India the first documented case of reincarnation was around 800 BCE. Investigating many different cultures, I've found that within most traditions there is some discussion about reincarnation. Off the top of my head are the Jews, early Christians, Egyptians, Buddhists, Alaskan Native Americans, those living in India, Igbo Nigeria, Cathars of France, and Hindu groups. In addition American Christians are believers. According to the Pew Research Center's 2009 forum on religion and public life, 24 percent of American Christians expressed a belief in reincarnation.

Digging into different cultures and religions for years I've concluded, there will always be some type of discussion about reincarnation. Once we complete this life and our "light" leaves our material body, reincarnation is a choice we can make.

In a 2010 article for *NY Jewish Week,* Rabbi Shmuly Yanklowitz discussed his embrace of reincarnation after first rejecting it as a non-Jewish theological belief. For Yanklowitz, adhering to this belief, with its theology of the interconnectedness of souls, opens the potential for a moral consciousness. We see that our lives are intertwined, and our reincarnation gives us the opportunity to make better choices and live a more moral existence:

> This belief [of reincarnation] is concerned with taking ownership of our complete existence. The moral enterprise of gilgulim (reincarnation) is concerned with our taking responsibility for the cultivation of the past, present, and future of our souls for our full transcendental ontological existence, our core being and deeper self.

These can include coming back to this material world to rectify our wrongs, learn other lessons, or perfect the soul. How could we discover all there is in one minuscule lifetime? Based on what we know about ourselves it might be interesting to make a list of these.

- Our unfinished business
- Dreams we haven't yet achieved
- Regrets and losses
- Life's deep disappointments
- Resentments
- Those we need to make peace with
- Damage we may have inflicted on others
- Harm inflicted upon us
- Heartaches
- Lingering anger or rage
- Unresolved grief
- Depression and sadness
- Our own sense of enlightenment

Is it possible that we have more lessons to learn and need other life experiences to achieve this? There is our spiritual state of mind to consider. How many of us truly believe we are spiritually or even intellectually perfect? We are diamonds, rubies, and emeralds in the rough. Maybe a few of us have been shaped and polished to a point where perfection has been achieved and are now flawless, but I can tell you for a fact that's not me. When people come into my office and they tell me they are perfect in every way, that everything is fine, I know something's up.

Over the last few years, I've had eight leg operations, one hip replacement, breast cancer, two dislocated hips, a cracked rib, and a few other things, all of which left me emotionally drained and crazy. Though I learned many incredible lessons, I also had to watch for resentment, irrational comments, displacement of anger, and other "falling off the cliff" disastrous deeds. Trust me, my personal ups and downs haven't always been graceful.

Am I a stronger soul for wading through all these challenges? Have I left the confining cocoon of hurt and blossomed into a better person, ready to gather new knowledge and experiences? Do I now have a better insight into others and myself? Am I now a polished diamond? For me to become a bit more refined, I believe I have a few more lives to live.

Yes, I'm like the butterfly and the silkworm, living one life of lessons and then moving into a cocoon of my own making, resting and preparing. At first this insulated environment may feel cozy, safe, and even comforting, but as I grow, this lifestyle is no longer helping me. It's time for a change in scenery. With pain and frustrating persistence, I escape the imprisonment of my cocoon to discover I'm free! Looking around I realize I'm a beautiful colorful spirit ready to lift my wings and fly off to the next journey.

TEN

Afterlife Experience as a Conduit to the Divine

Beyond Religious Abuse

We feel and know that we are eternal.

—BARUCH SPINOZA, *ETHICS*, PART 5, PROP. 23

Baruch Spinoza (1632–1677), who's name in Hebrew means "breath," grew up in a Sephardic Jewish home and community (no potato latkes, I'll take rice). As the boy grew into a young man, he gradually moved away from the god and traditions of his youth. During his early adult years, Spinoza was a merchant, importing dried fruit and meeting various people from all walks of life. This could have cracked the door open for the Age of Enlightenment.

During this Renaissance, philosophers, artists, musicians, writers, poets, and other free thinkers exploded onto the stage and let loose their ideas and creativity. Spinoza relished the thought of being a part of these like-minded groups where debate was expected. Within these new circles he wouldn't be called a heretic or censured for having ideas of his own.

A Trip to an Italian Grocery Store

While looking for Italian plums in Italy, I was almost locked out of a small neighborhood grocery store. I discovered wanting an Italian plum was an outrageous request. Then I told the clerk I always bought Italian plums when in Italy and had been waiting to get my hands on some for a while. By now my mouth was aching for the taste of this fruit. Seeing my request was not going to be fulfilled I threw up my hands up in the air and went to another store not far from the first grocery. Here questions like mine were not pushed aside. They had Italian plums grown in Italy. A few store workers did disagree with me on just how flavorful the Italian plum was, adding there were also Japanese plums, Victoria plums, czar plums, or friar plums. And as the conversation continued, we all loudly quibbled about mushrooms, tomatoes, eggplant, artichokes, pasta, and sausage. It was a good time.

So goes the way of those philosophers dedicated to asking questions about God, spirituality, or cocreating with something much larger and more powerful than ourselves. For each seeker, Jewish or not, the goal has always been the same. Even though the path may look a bit different, the freedom to express one's thoughts is what's of most importance. The need for spiritual growth and exploration is the same across most of the board, and hopefully there will always be a place for debate and argument. The primary news flash is that no one needs to be kicked out of the debate. They might be yelled out, but free thinkers will not show anyone the door. Did I tell you I eventually tried a Japanese plum?

The Dutch Jews Excommunicate Spinoza

In 1656 the Jews of Amsterdam made a terrible decision. No, they did not decide to turn over the hash trade to other European Jewish merchants. Instead, they did something much worse: they excommunicated the twenty-three-year-old Baruch Spinoza from the Amsterdam syna-gogue. That's right, Baruch Spinoza, the brilliant seventeenth-century philosopher and one of the founders of modern thought and illumina-tion, was given the boot. And why was he removed? Spinoza received a severe and merciless expulsion from Amsterdam's Jewish elite for chal-lenging the Judaic thought of the time, expressing his philosophical ideas about God, and not keeping his opinions to himself. This was before any of his views on paper had made it to the print shop.

The poor guy was cursed in every manner. Wanting to believe in a god that made sense to him, Spinoza had become more argumenta-tive with the Jews of Amsterdam. He also felt he needed to talk about his thoughts openly within his Jewish community. Instead, his writings were banned for all of eternity. That's right! All eternity!

Because he was expressing himself, he was shown the door, and the gate was slammed with a loud thunder. The shunning of both his intel-lectual and physical person had to have hurt. I know I'd even feel hos-tile if this happened to me. Eventually, Spinoza would find a group of like-minded peers with whom he could speak his mind without being emotionally bludgeoned to death.

WHO INITIALLY PRIED OPEN THE MIND OF SPINOZA?

Rabbi Nachmanides (1194–1270), Spinoza's mentor, was born in Spain, centuries before Spinoza. A well-respected Talmudist, Sephardic Jew, rabbi, pragmatist, physician, and philosopher, he had already laid down a foundation for those abandoned by their one-time heroes. He spent most of his life in Spain, but once he was seventy years old, he too was pushed out of his own country.

Like Spinoza, Rabbi Nachmanides also found himself in hot water for speaking his mind. And just what did he say? Nachmanides believed that the Torah had many untapped otherworldly ideas to offer.

According to Rabbi Gil Student, in an article for Orthodox Union, Nachmanides believed that "people in the Afterlife have souls and bodies, just like we do in this world."

Can you imagine the bad will and fireworks he set off when he openly talked about such concepts? Such conversations were not tolerated because this involved debate, and debate creates the birth of differing views, consisting of a multitude of voices questioning their views on religion. Why were the privileged so bent on keeping the public ignorant from such fascinating thoughts? Leaders of these communities had an investment in maintaining control of the population. Openly discussing such notions as an afterlife or life after death would have pulled the populace away from those in control. No longer frightened by governing heads of state or the religiously narrow-minded, society would have felt safe exploring new ideas. Sadly, for those thinking outside the box, expression wasn't going to make any dent in the wall. Too many Jewish philosophers equaled too many opinions. Too many opinions would have resulted in a loss of financial control, and for those in power, this was too much to even think about.

Because of Nachmanides, Spinoza received his introduction to the unseen world. Spinoza then went on to influence philosophers across different parts of the world.

SCHILLER ON LIFE AFTER DEATH

One philosopher who picked up on the words and work of Spinoza was German-British philosopher F. C. S. Schiller (1864–1937). Schiller also explored and was very influenced by the work of American philosopher and psychologist William James (1842–1910), known as the father of psychology. He became a leading British pragmatist philosopher (a practical person who thinks and acts along the lines of practicality) during the early 1900s. Schiller was also a supporter of evolution. Yes, he was a freethinker. Though both his father and mother were born in Calcutta, Schiller's life took place at different locations around the world.

Below, Schiller clearly expresses what he thought about his peers' reaction to views on life after death (from *Humanism: Philosophical Essays*).

Death is a topic on which philosophers have been astonishingly commonplace. Spinoza was right in maintaining that there is no subject concerning which the sage thinks less than about death which never the less is a great piety for the sage as surely wrong there is no subject concerning which he, if he is an idealist and has the courage of his opinion, ought to think more and ought to have more interesting things to say.

Before his death, Schiller, who had written his first works under a false name for fear of reprisal from his peers, wrote a work titled *Must Philosophers Disagree and Other Essays in Popular Philosophy*. I believe it's a must-read for anyone seriously interested in studying philosophy. Philosophers create upheaval with one another, and with this the expansion of the mind can take place. Stale thinking can turn the brain into rot. A desire for a fresher look, which can take us to the edge, where new ideas and openmindedness live, can be found.

Skeptics and certain members of the public have always put up roadblocks against all sorts of new ideas. The motivation is fear, the dread of looking directly at what we thought was right, and then realizing there just might be some flaws in our thinking. Here is where healthy debate can happen.

MY FATHER-IN-LAW'S REJECTION OF RELIGION

At the end of the war, my French father-in-law led the allies through the streets of Paris, assessing damage. My father-in-law was the only person who knew the layout of the city. He saw many individuals who had been destroyed by war. Along with this he went searching for all the relatives who were still in the camps. I can't even imagine what he saw. It had to be gruesome and heartbreaking.

When my father-in-law returned home to France, he discovered that most of his family had died in the Holocaust. He became a physician, more specifically an eye surgeon. The French made the decision to kick all undesirables out of the country, and he learned he was considered an undesirable because he had attended a Communist Party lecture in his youth.

His sister moved to Israel, while he and my mother-in-law decided to create a life again in the States. My mother-in-law contacted relatives who were already living in the States and asked if they could assist them in leaving France. My mother-in-law left her mother, father, brother, and sister in Poland in order to be with her husband.

After setting down new roots, my father-in-law joined the U.S. Army. As a surgeon he cared for Holocaust survivors and soldiers who had been mangled and lost limbs while fighting on the front lines. After my father-in-law reopened his eye surgery clinic in the states, he started employing immigrants from various parts of Europe and Eastern Europeans who had survived the war. These individuals, who at one time were doctors, academics, and dentists, were willing to take any type of job. He was very good to them.

Then with the Cold War he started to look for relatives in Russia and was able to relocate several of them to the United States. Slowly my in-laws made it to the States. They found a community of Jewish people who they could associate with. These friends remained close to my father- and mother-in-law till their dying days. This community in the United States made the sting of leaving the homeland less painful.

We all knew my father-in-law had Nazi German handguns in the attic, but we were surprised to discover a collection of yellow Stars of David after his death. He never talked about the war, and when such conversations would come up, he would leave the room. My father-in-law had seen firsthand the best in humanity and the worst. Being in Europe before and after the war must have been an emotionally and spiritually damaging experience. One can only imagine the destruction and pain he'd witnessed or experienced. He never talked about any of this. The way my father-in-law survived the gruesome memories of the Holocaust was by staying away from synagogues and by letting us all know he was an agnostic.

I Became My Father-in-Law

The history was a crushing burden and has to some extent paralyzed me.

—Rita Goldberg, second-generation
Holocaust survivor

One year I found myself traveling to an old mill house situated along a rushing river. The purpose for this trip was to meet with famous near-death experience researcher Raymond A. Moody Jr., M.D. I was interested in hearing what his take was on life after physical death.

Around this same time, I had an extremely harsh moment with a famous rabbi. I'd shared with him intimate details about my childhood only to have my experiences negated. This rabbi started to compare, in an unflattering way, my abuses with the murder of six million Jews—forgetting that the Holocaust had impacted several generations in my family. My issues were extremely painful, but I wasn't allowed to openly discuss them because my plight would then be compared to the Holocaust.

I couldn't get out of that temple fast enough. At that point I really needed healthy, spiritual council. This was the last straw. The matzah had broken into a thousand pieces. The shame for sharing about my abuse began to submerge me into darkness, and it took another decade for me to face it again. For several years after this, I had no interest in exploring my history.

Over time I started to become a mirror image of my father-in-law. The dread and fear of the holidays along with other celebrations soaked my soul with anxiety. The consequences of how war and loss had left many relatives very damaged. This pain trickled on down the generations, and it had to be buried. "If I can't fix the inside, I will never look at such events again. Instead, I will glamorize the outside."

So, I left Judaism to get my feelings and thoughts grounded. For answers to my questions, I turned to freethinkers who were open to exploring questions like: "Is death the end?" "Will I see my deceased relatives and friends when I die?" "What happens to me after I die? Do I just evaporate into the stratosphere?"

My journey started with a circle of like-minded people in 1984 in Taos, New Mexico. Young, old, all genders and religious backgrounds congregated in the snowy high mountains to look at and embrace new ideas. I jumped into the experience very quickly. What I experienced was a real eye-opener. This included walking on hot coals (no, my feet were never burned), meditation in the snowy mountains (my husband fell asleep on top of a rock), rappelling off large cliffs, and participation in a traditional Indian prayer ceremony in a sweat lodge. My Taos adventure exposed me to ideas foreign to what I'd grown up with. After a week, I left the mountains more confused than ever. A few concepts were baking away, but crystallization was going to take a while.

How Concepts of God, Religion, and Spirituality Develop in Childhood

At the beginning of childhood, we first learn about who we are by watching our parents. We discover what it means to be male by observing our fathers. Most young boys try to act like their dads by attempting to talk, stand, walk, and sit like their dad. Here we have the initial stages of modeling. Little girls may also try to act like their fathers. For me this involved trying on aftershave cologne, stepping into his boots, and clopping around or by just being tough. Young girls discover who they are by watching their mothers. I remember getting into my mom's cosmetic drawer. Not knowing what I was doing, I tried on her lipsticks and, unsuccessfully, her eyeshadow and face powder. Of course, role-playing by dressing up in my mother's clothes with other boys and girls was a weekend must. One day the girls and boys switched roles. That was quite the event!

Because children depend on caretakers for food, clothing, shelter, nurturing, and more, parents represent survival. As a result of this, children also see their parents as all-knowing, and godlike. As a matter of fact, our first concept of a higher power or God comes from our perception of our parents or caretakers, not our religion. Our initial concept of a godlike figure usually has many of the characteristics our parents possess. It would be very scary for a child to know all the imperfections adults can possess. Children depend on caretakers to keep them safe.

When a child is physically abused by an adult, that adult is behaving irresponsibly and is not handling his or her anger properly. Physical abuse is a destructive expression of anger and depression. Many of us carry a great deal of rage and fear from experiencing physical abuse as a child. If we try to ignore childhood emotional, physical, sexual, and spiritual abuse, this will bite us on the backside. Our feelings are not bad, but if we were punished as children for expressing emotion, this can impact us for the rest of our lives. When we sidestep our feelings about this, we may find, as adults, that we misdirect our feelings onto family, friends, workplace peers, and others.

When we leave home, we may shed a few tears, but most of us are ready to start living our own lives. All appears to be going well until we hit our first serious relationship! "I always told myself I'd never have a relationship like my parents." Is this you? Not being like our parents is more than clothes, music, friends, career, and emotional expression. This can also be religion and spiritual beliefs. Healthy spirituality and sexuality have both lived in a closet of shame throughout history because of lack of information. Religion can also play a big part in how we feel about ourselves and the world around us.

We also discover what relationships are by watching to see how our parents interact with each other. Was there respect, compromise, fair fighting, fun, the ability to weather through the rough times, and appreciation for each other's differences? Watching how each parent or partner behaves with the other is an essential part of our relational foundation. Such foundations can have a powerful impact on learning more about ourselves.

Children are naturally self-centered and believe the world rotates around them. This viewpoint and behavior are normal and are a natural part of child development. When we get older and decide to have children, we can find ourselves trying to discipline these young ones with religion. Most likely we didn't receive a healthy dose of spirituality ourselves; we may have been shamed, disciplined, and even abused by our parents and other figures of authority, such as a rabbi, with the result that we perpetuate the same on our children.

RELIGIOUS ADDICTION AND ABUSE

Religious addiction involves the obsessive use of religion, literature, or punishment in the name of God, or using God when disciplining. Using any other deity as a means of humiliation or for fear-inducing purposes is an abuse of religion and spiritually damaging. Religious addiction usually entails self-righteousness.

This is a sneaky addiction in many respects. All may look great on the outside, when there is a nightmare brewing in the closet. As a means of escaping feelings, avoiding reality, and justifying inappropriate behavior, religious addiction serves a purpose. Religious obsession is frequently found within unhealthy family systems. The purpose for this is a need to control. Even with the sense of public disgrace associated with addiction, family loss, or disappointment, in the eyes of the religious addict, excessive self-righteousness (the addiction) will right the wrong.

There was a rabbi who began a series of sexual affairs with females within a Jewish congregation. The damage done was incredibly destructive for the women and men in the congregation and community. When confronted about his behavior the rabbi flipped and began blaming all his victims for these affairs. Because he was in a position of power and authority, he abused his spiritual station a second time by insinuating that the women were not reliable and possibly mentally ill.

The religious addict or offender can be very good at pointing the finger at people they have victimized, by blaming them for the abuse. The addict can twist around whatever the other person does or says. These individuals will go to any lengths to justify their behavior. The addict will use denial, rationalization, slander, and delusional thinking to vilify a victim. In doing this the offender believes his or her offensive behavior is perfectly acceptable. Those who have been abused may try to speak up, only to hear: "This person [the addict, offender, abuser] is such a devout Jew. The family is very prominent in the community. How could you make such accusations? The family really embraces Judaism and works hard at helping others. What a horrible thing to say!" The result is victims can feel very crazy and find themselves questioning reality.

For those abused by clergy the consequences are devastating. Clergy members are the teachers of spiritual principles and are perceived as a connection to God or a higher power. They are trusted servants and spiritual directors within their communities. They are in a position of power regarding spiritual matters. Sadly, a few bad apples can ruin it for everyone else.

What I first hear from many of those who have been abused is: "How could God let him abuse me? He's a rabbi, priest, minister, nun, preacher, our spiritual leader. Shouldn't he or she know better? Doesn't God love me?"

Some parents will also keep the victimization a secret. Telling children, adolescents, or adult children to never speak of the incident is shaming for the victims. If we want to heal, we must share the unacceptable sexual or other abusive behavior with someone like a well-vetted therapist, trusted friend, recommended clergy or teacher, or trustworthy family member.

Unfortunately, religious addiction complicates hidden secrets, abuse, trauma, neglect, and more. When an addict pulls in other people and makes promises in an attempt to wipe his or her slate clean, this can lay a foundation for enablers. Those others can enable addicts by pulling for them or fighting for their unhealthy causes or shielding them. Such individuals have been led to believe they are righteously doing a good deed or getting something out of protecting the individual who is causing harm.

DEPARTING LIGHT

Rabbi Israel Baal Shem Tov was a famous historical scholar who founded the Hasidic branch of Judaism in the eighteenth century. As he was preparing to pass, he spoke to his followers about how his soul was leaving his body. They were surprised to witness their rabbi's departure. According to Buber (*Tales of the Hasidim*): "When he was buried, his followers said they saw his soul head toward the heavens in the form of a blue flame."

Down through the centuries, those at the bedside of a dying loved one have reported seeing mists, light, and body doubles leaving the body. This phenomenon continues today. My cousin was by her mother's side when she departed from the physical world. At the moment of death, she saw a silver mist leaving her mother's body.

Even the helping profession is beginning to open and share what they have witnessed with their dying patients or grandparents. In my book *One Last Hug before I Go,* I recorded the account of a nurse who sat watching a dying patient as he prepared to join his physically deceased friends and loved ones. She observed his last breath: "Surrendering his last breath, I saw a beautiful silvery and blue light. . . . It was his soul, his spirit exiting his body."

This can be a great healing event for all. Profound life changes can occur from the youngest to the most senior. Here we have spirituality at its best. When our loved ones leave the material world this is not the final good-bye. The only thing that changes is how we communicate. Sadly, some of the remarks made by physicians to patients or their family members are often cold, insensitive, or very trivializing. In spite of this more medical people are having and reporting their own afterlife accounts.

Physicians can be a very difficult crowd to deal with. This is usually about them and their history. It appears the need to be popped over the head with a turquoise-colored foam baseball bat might be a must for this group. Thankfully, this is not always the case.

In my book *Heavenly Hugs: Comfort, Support, and Hope from the Afterlife,* I recount the story of a team of surgeons in Stockholm struggling to save the life of a plane crash victim. Despite their best efforts, the man died. The anesthesiologist present, Dr. Jan Lundquist, described what happened:

Everything happened so suddenly and quickly that I sometimes wonder if I just imagined it. But I didn't just imagine it. We all saw it—a dazzling misty-blue light that came right out of that body and floated upward and then just seemed to dissolve like a stream into nothing. I wasn't surprised at all that the patient died. He was in a terrible state. The surgeons did everything they could. But even as they worked, I knew we were losing him. Suddenly every vital sign ceased. All life signs stopped. There was just a deep hollow moaning sound and I looked up to tell the surgeons that our patient was gone. That's when I saw an incredible shimmering light. Right before our eyes that glowing vapor rose. Somehow, I was watching the soul leave the mortal remains of the man who lay before me.

This event not only turned the head of the anesthesiologist but also the three surgeons, six nurses, and four technicians present.

PREMONITIONS:
SENSING, HEARING, TASTING, DREAMING

Mist and light aren't the only by product of a physical passing. Premonitions of an upcoming travel to the afterlife takes place more often than we think. When my aunt was gearing up to make her journey to the next world, I didn't know I'd had a premonition. When I walked into her bedroom, I sensed something was different. Though there were only a few present, the room felt very crowded. Semitransparent images of many deceased loved ones drinking, eating, and even gossiping felt very natural. The fragrant smell of family foods was there. I then sensed that these relatives were here for her, waiting to escort this aunt to the other side. Another woman present said she too had sensed the same thing.

In the following story, Ruth's friend visits her and seems to foretell his own death.

Ruth's Premonition
Ruth F.

It's 1972, my senior year at college. I am living with a couple of other women in Little Italy in Cleveland, Ohio. I have a dream in which I am asleep in my apartment when there is a knock on the door. The door to the apartment opens into the kitchen, and the fridge is on my right as I open the door. My friend Charley is standing there looking his normal disheveled nerdy self, wearing his orange winter jacket. He comes in and tells me how hungry he is. I tell him to help himself to whatever he wants in the fridge, but tell him that I'm going back to bed and to make sure he locks the door behind him. When I open the fridge for him, it is very bright inside and totally empty except for a bowl of eggs, which I assume are hard boiled. The dream ends.

The next morning when I am just waking up and musing about the dream, there is a knock at the door. When I open it my friend Chris, who is Charley's suite roommate, is standing there and tells me that Charley committed suicide during the night.

Ruth sees her friend in a dream, and he has come asking for a meal. Upon opening the refrigerator, all she can see is a bright golden light with a few eggs. In many traditions, eggs represent the circle of life. Judaism is no different. We have birth and celebration followed by death and mourning.

Eggs are often eaten by Jews during mourning. According to the website Mishpacha ("Judaism and Death"), this first meal "often consists of bread and hard-boiled eggs. Eggs represent the circle of life, the cycle of birth and death. Ashes are often sprinkled on the egg to represent grief and loss."

The bright golden light described in Ruth's visitation is commonly reported in many near-death experiences and departing visions. The next morning Ruth discovers her friend has committed suicide. Was his dream visitation a warning? In any case, individuals can provide messages before, during, or after they physically pass.

Benjamin Netanyahu, love him or hate him, is the first Israeli-born prime minister. He's also been elected three times, the last time in 2022. Though a war hero and well-known political leader, how many of us are aware that Netanyahu had a premonition of his brother's death before he was killed?

On July 4, 1976, Netanyahu learned Israelite Defense Force or IDF soldiers had landed in Entebbe, Uganda, for a rescue mission. Netanyahu knew his brother must be there. Yoni was an Israeli Defense Forces officer. After the premonition, Netanyahu called his parents.

At the time, the future prime minister was twenty-six years old and attending MIT in the United States. When he received a telephone call from brother Iddo, he immediately knew his brother Yoni was dead. At age thirty, he had died in combat during the Entebbe rescue mission. The purpose of the undertaking was to free hostages being held by Palestinian and German revolutionary terrorists on an Air France airliner. The prime minister has since visited the Entebbe airport where his beloved brother Yoni was killed.

Yoni was the only IDF soldier killed in action. During the raid over one hundred Israelis and Jews were rescued from an Air France jetliner. Because of Yoni's tragic death and the terrorism impacting Israel, Netanyahu felt his calling was politics. In a *New York Times* interview, Netanyahu told journalists Jeffrey Gettleman and Isabel Kershner that, when he has to dispatch people to dangerous places, "it's in times like these that I consult with my brother—and they're a lot more frequent than you might think."

Rene Hope Turner, through a near-death experience, had a premonition of her grandmother's death. Turner was raised Jewish, with all holidays observed. After receiving a doctorate in biblical literature history and a bachelor of science in mechanical optical engineering, she then made Australia her home, where she purchased forest property and with the timber built a house. I communicated with her years ago and can tell you she is one resourceful woman.

Enjoying life and feeling content, a tragic car accident suddenly put Turner in a coma. Her doctor even told her parents she was dead. As the neurosurgeon continued to insist that she had indeed passed on, a very excited nurse reported Turner had suddenly sat up in bed and was talking! Once conscious, she began recalling memories during her time in a coma. Not only did she meet up with her deceased grandfather, but he also had an important message for her about an event that was soon to come. Her account of her experience appeared in a 2019 article in the website Near-Death Experiences and the Afterlife ("Dr. Rene Turner's Near Death Experience" by Kevin Williams), of which a portion is given below:

> There coming towards me was my grandfather. He looked younger than I remembered and was without his hare lip or cleft pallet, but undoubtedly my grandfather. We hugged. . . .
> Granddad told me that grandma was coming soon and he was looking forward to her arrival.

Three months later her grandmother was diagnosed with an untreatable illness and passed not long after this. In this account three generations are brought together. A deceased grandfather comes to his granddaughter, not only to offer reassurance but also to let her know her grandmother would soon be dying. Though Turner's mother was upset upon hearing this, the awareness just might have softened the hurt grief can bring. The care and love a father and grandfather had for his daughter and granddaughter moved from the afterlife to the present.

HEAVENLY CALLING CARDS

Speaking of parents, can they still parent us even if they are no longer in the material world? I've always believed that hearing is the last sense to go before we physically die. Will the dearly departed quit talking to us just because they are no longer in human form? My aunt Helen says, "Of course not. When will you ever learn?" Rabbi Benjamin Blech, author of *Hope, Not Fear: Changing the Way We View Death,* recounted the following story to journalist Jonathan Mark, a clear example of deceased parents helping their children:

> I had someone in my shul who was a bombardier in World War II. He was flying in combat and heard his father who was dead, call his name. The son turned. A bullet whizzed by. The son would have been shot if he hadn't heard (his father).

An even more powerful story is that of Esther Raab, whose deceased mother helped her escape a Nazi death camp. Raab (1922–2015), a survivor of the Holocaust, was born in Chelm, Poland. Raab has given several interviews about those terrifying times and always speaks honestly.

In 1942 she was taken to Sobibor, a killing center in occupied Poland. There she worked in a barracks sorting the clothing and possessions of people gassed at the camp. A year later she and several hundred others planned an uprising and escape.

The night before the escape, she had a dream about her deceased mother. In the dream, her mother told her that upon escaping Sobibor to look for a certain barn that belonged to Christian friends of the family. After running from the camp, she and two other escapees found the barn she had dreamed about and she discovered—wonder of wonders— that her brother, Yidel, who she thought had been murdered by Nazis, was in the barn. Yidel had built into the barn a bunker where he and his sister hid and survived the war.

Raab and her husband, Irving, eventually made their way to America in 1950. The couple moved to Vineland, New Jersey, and had a son named Abraham. An after-death dream communication between mother and daughter saved Esther Raab and her family's legacy.

Our calling card in this life is often our calling card in the next. I have always believed and sensed that those in the afterlife will present themselves to us in a recognizable manner. So, if my mother had blonde hair in the material world, she's not necessarily going to show up to me living in an afterlife with pink or bright-blue hair.

Often, I tell people that they are just lining up to be with us. Those in the afterlife want to talk to us as much as we may want to talk to them. Twenty years ago, I had a dream. I saw all sorts of different faces trying to get through a tiny door. Oh, how they struggled. At that moment I knew they were individuals who loved me, protected me, and continued to teach me lessons from another world. This went on for about a month.

Our loved ones will do whatever they need to do to get a message to us, whether it's through dreams, premonitions, afterlife communications, or any other type of contact. Most of the time it is we who are not listening, seeing, smelling, or sensing. Something will happen and we may just blow it off to our imagination. When we do this and refuse to look at an explanation, we are closing the door on a possible connection with the afterlife.

They will not stop. We can't make them angry, and there is no reason to be frightened of them. As we have seen, these sorts of experiences have been going on since ancient times. And they had been documented up to modern times. Individuals have written entire books about after-death communications or departing visions or messages through dreams. Know there are no veils or doors or rivers or ponds separating us and this world from those in the next world.

Somewhere along the way we became frightened and turned toward what seems like safe dogma. Though we were told what to believe, and it seemed interesting, but debate was only accepted to a certain point. New ideas were squandered, and many of us became somewhat stale.

Moldy Bread, Our Choice

Look at that moldy rotten piece of bread.
Blue, green and black in color.
And oh, that smell!

> *It beckons us to take a bite.*
> *One more time.*
> *Should we or should we not?*
> *We already know what it tastes like.*
>
> —Carla Wills-Brandon

ELEVEN

We Are Not Alone . . .
And It's a Good Thing

Death has never been a one-way trip. On your travels carry a couple of bagels with you.

—CARLA WILLS-BRANDON

Over the years I've continued to investigate unusual activity at not only Nazi death camps like Auschwitz in Poland, Theresienstadt (also known as Terezin) in the Czech Republic, and Russian gulags in Siberia, but also at various World War II sites, places of tragedy and historical battlefields. I had my share of unusual experiences at these spots and have listened to tourists, along with Holocaust survivors, speak of encountering spirit activity or hearing unseen voices at these locations. One of the descriptive words used repeatedly is *unnerving*.

Over the decades people walking the grounds of Auschwitz have reported that their cameras stopped working when they attempted to take pictures of the hair removed from the heads of prisoners, displayed in a room, one of the most gruesome scenes I've ever been confronted with. There were also mysterious, unearthly, otherworldly encounters, which had the feeling of consciousness. Visitors have

165

reported feeling small invisible hands slip into theirs. Voices with no visible origin have been heard as visitors have made their way into the sleeping quarters.

SHADOWY SOULS AND TRAGIC LOOPS

I will never forget my trip to Auschwitz concentration camp. Joining a handful of relatives, all of us were silent as we drove from Krakow to the notorious death camp. Being there with my aunt who was an actual survivor of three Nazi death camps, including Auschwitz, was life changing and a moment in time I will never forget.

It was bone-chilling cold, and the sun could not be found. The atmosphere at Auschwitz felt like condensed darkness, murky gloom, physical sickness, and death. We slowly trudged into dark cold barracks, saw drab rows of open toilets, spent time in gas chambers, and were saddened to see the concrete rooms filled with the personal belongings of each victim imprisoned in the camp. To this day, I remember sobbing when I went up to a glass window where I saw piled high used Zyklon B or cyanide cans, the poison used to gas millions of those in the death camps. Along with this was another room stacked high with luggage. Almost all these suitcases had the names of victimized owners scrawled across them.

I walked into the expansive barnlike barracks that had been set up for prisoners to sleep, cook, and wash their ragged clothing. I have no words to describe what I was feeling. There was a deafening silence and a forbidding sense about these places. Quietly moving through the dank, chilly rooms where prisoners had slept in very tight quarters left me feeling disheartened and sad. I could see dozens of ethereal, emaciated women pushed together on wooden boards. I sensed loops of energy and watched as four shadowy Holocaust figures lay down upon the rough wooden planks, their movements played repeatedly, bruising my soul. The loops continued to play out the tragedies, but there wasn't any deliberate connection. It was like watching a movie with the projector stuck on one scene.

A loop is like a play where the actors have no awareness, inner emotion, or connectedness to what's really going on. It's an imprint of history, of extreme emotion and energy, onto a location. With a loop, there isn't any feeling or personal conscious contact or sense of interaction to be found. The loop just tells a story with no life attached to it. With a loop there can be an extreme sense of heaviness. The environment has sucked in a tragedy, which now plays continuously at the same location repeatedly, where it first occurred.

ACTIVE CONSCIOUSNESS AND ORBS

I sensed not only the loops in these buildings but also an active form of consciousness. While in the death camp quarters I felt something brushing the front of my neck. This interactive contact going both ways between the physically dead and living can feel like a normal conversation.

Once home, I happened upon several photographs I had taken in the sleeping quarters and the communal toilets that had translucent orbs. I remembered walking around the toilets when I felt something brushing the front of my face several times. A source of light for the round dancing orbs could not be directly found. The spectacles and suitcases are in separate rooms. Though the scenes were horrific the active activity of the orbs just might provide a bit of peace to the souls who remain.

In an article on the website Real Paranormal Experiences called "Are There Ghosts in Auschwitz?" the author writes that "orbs and strange shapes have been recorded dancing about the mangled mounds of broken spectacles and redundant, battered suitcases." To see orbs around Nazi death camps suggests this is conscious contact.

Nurses, hospice workers, and family members have reported

seeing small orbs at the moment of the death of a patient or loved one, among them the mother-daughter writing team, Elise Lowers and Julene Anderson, who report their experiences in *Orbs: The Untold Story*. Virginia M. Hummel describes in her book *Orbs and the Afterlife* how, months after the death of her twenty-five-year-old son, Christopher, she witnessed an orb: "One night, 20 months after my son's death, a brilliant ball of light the size of a ping pong ball appeared in my darkened bedroom. It darted across the room, made a sharp left, darted another six or eight feet and disappeared." For Hummel, the appearance of that orb and others that she saw later was validation that we survive death and connection is possible with loved ones who have died.

Orbs are a curious wonder, and they continue to be debated to this day. Are these moving balls of light a loop or conscious contact? Because I have seen these transparent spheres with my own eyes in photographs, on videotape, and while using face-to-face technologies such as Zoom, Skype, Face Time, I believe that there is something to this phenomenon. While doing a Skype session with somebody, I suddenly saw two translucent white silvery spheres of light traveling different paths, up and down across my computer screen. One appeared a little smaller than the other, and both had characteristics of others I'd seen.

In 2009 a man in the U.S. Army and stationed in Germany reported the following experience on the website Your Ghost Stories:

My wife and I recently took a trip to Dachau Concentration Camp in Munich. . . . My wife and I walked to the old crematory. There were stories how people were tortured. As we walked in, I was taking pictures, and as my wife walked in she almost passed out and had a severe headache. After we walked out, it went away. I took some pictures inside there and you could see two small orbs in the picture.

Orbs can appear at any time. You don't have to be a clairvoyant to see them. Nor does the appearance of these orbs only happen in the dark. I have seen them in sunny daylight and nighttime. The ones I've had contact with are mostly bluish-white or white in color. Occasionally I'll see orbs that are silver gray. One time a friend of mine who is also interested in this topic took several pictures of orbs. He picked up one photograph in particular and expanded it so we could get a better look. The sphere appeared to have a face in it. By expanding photographs of orbs, faces often appear. I'm not the only one who has seen this. Let's look closely at what an orb may be composed of.

A 2012 article on the website Ocprstoronto ("Orbs: The Souls of the Dead?" by Demetrius) provides this definition of orb: "the spherical shape of a soul or spirit; is thought be comprised of a mass of some form of energy. Orbs are translucent, and the sizes of Orbs vary. They appear in photographs and video recording devices."

People always ask me if Jews can see orbs. My answer to this is "of course!": there are a multitude of examples of this phenomenon found in books, photographs, firsthand accounts, documentations, movies, stories, and videos. Just like within other religions and even with skeptics, this phenomenon has been witnessed by those of every religion and around the world. Aside from my own experiences, I have also examined the subject as presented by experts in the field. What is most interesting are the accounts given by those seeing an orb for the first time.

Though most orbs are of a bluish, silver, or white-gray color, I've also seen all sorts of colored orbs. When I went through the photographs I had taken at Auschwitz, one orb caught my eye. A pink, blue, and purple sphere was high up in the far-right corner of one of the gas chambers. Along with many relatives, my husband's grandmother died in an Auschwitz gas chamber. As we both looked at this orb, we were overwhelmed with emotion. Some investigators, the aforementioned

Demetrius, think that each color represents a certain emotion or characteristic.

Colors aren't the only characteristics that have been reported. As I said earlier there are those who scoff and proclaim all of this is gobbledygook, that this is just the product of dust, moisture, or camera dysfunction. This may be, but I ask, please, try to keep an open mind. The majority of these photos could just be dirt floating through the air, but then there are others that don't fit the description. We can't be so black and white.

As stated, most orbs have certain characteristics in common, round and slivery, whitish, or blue in color. Then there are other light forms that can appear on photographs. These are called vectors. A vector of light can often be found running in a semi or diagonal direction in a thick, straight line across an individual's body. They can also appear behind the person being photographed or in front of the individual. What I find so incredibly interesting is that the color of these vectors are typically a bright white. Sometimes they appear to be wispy clouds around the individual. Most people don't notice this while they're taking the picture but afterward are often shocked to see these vectors show up.

Over the years I've taken numerous photos of my sons. A few months ago, I was putting these into an album. While doing this I discovered a few vectors. These occurrences allegedly imply protective light is near. Throughout the years I've taken rolls of pictures of both my sons. Interestingly I've found two with long vectors of light diagonally crossing my youngest son's body. One photo was taken in Taos, New Mexico, and another in our home on the Texas Gulf. While taking these photos, at the time I didn't see any vectors. But upon studying these photographs, the thick white lines were difficult to ignore. I have never gone looking for orbs and vectors, but they sure seem to find me! Though they may come to us, we can miss the moment if we aren't vigilant.

Looking at Loops and Consciousness in Scotland

About a decade ago my family and I were back in Scotland, and we went to Culloden Moor, Inverness. It is here that the last major Scottish war for independence from the British took place. The site was full of mounds. Walking the moors, I learned that each mound contained the remains of soldiers who had fought and died in this war. When I discovered this, I understood why all my senses were firing away at once. I had been walking across the remnants or graves of thousands of Scottish Jacobite Soldiers.

During my hike I encountered the consciousness of those souls who were still trying to sort out their war history. They would turn to gaze at me and then either smile, salute me directly, appear unhappy, or nod. After acknowledging their presence, these souls returned to their tasks. This was not a loop, as some of them even waved at me. It was interactive consciousness. We had communicated with one another. They live in one form of consciousness while I exist in another.

As I made my way over the mounds of the battlefield, I suddenly realized I just now might be in a loop. Driving past wooded areas in North Carolina, I sometimes hear, sense, and vaguely see British redcoats racing through the woods. This is another loop. I've witnessed the same scene play repeatedly on earlier trips in North Carolina.

Grandfather the Fixer

My grandfather and I had a special relationship. We talked about many things, and he also taught me how to change a flat tire. But then there were those family secrets that were taboo. He was of a generation where one rarely talked about closeted topics, especially to those who had struggled to make it to the United States. My grandfather's mother passed when he was just sixteen. I've always thought he put up with my antics because we were both motherless at the age of sixteen. In the early days, he and his family, an ethnic group, were referred to by a name that had many racist undertones. We had grown up with similar childhoods.

When my grandfather crossed over, I was absolutely devastated. He had been my rock. Don't get me wrong. My grandfather had his own fears to battle. When it came to our relationship, I had always felt safe. Sadly, there was always bad blood between me and some of the other family members. This went on for about forty years. Can you imagine? Having such emotion with no resolution in sight? Yes, that's the way it was. So, for the next decades I wept in silence.

A few years later I was diagnosed with breast cancer. Thank goodness the family rules had already begun to change. A door had cracked open slightly. Slowly over time family relationships improved. In my private clinical practice, I have watched people go to their graves desperately hating someone or something. In other words, they hold one another hostage with loud or silent rage. Nothing is resolved, and the future looks bleak. To try to brush away the wreckage of the past is like attempting to push a bunch of bubble wrap into a teeny tiny box. No matter how hard we try, the will of the bubble wrap creates chaos and powerlessness.

Recently I received a birthday call. I would have never thought this individual would have picked up the phone to call me. It was a good conversation. Then suddenly, I felt my grandfather. I'd had a sense of his presence. He had made his trip to the afterlife over thirty years ago. But suddenly there he was, grateful that this relationship had been mended. Very grateful. He had spent so many years trying to fix the broken bond between me and other family members and would say, "It doesn't have to be this way." This was not a loop. This was conscious communication from my grandfather in an afterlife to me in the material world.

"Never say never" is a wisdom I carry around with me daily. In my clinical practice I've watched too many people continue to despise a relative or friend. Yes, painful wounds must be healed. Leaving any wreckage of the past, unfinished and unaddressed, is like having a barbed wire fence separating us from each other.

What I've learned is that trauma in this world can be healed. My interaction with my grandfather was not a loop. This was conscious communication. A very unexpected, out-of-the blue experience. He had never appeared to me like this before.

REDEMPTION THROUGH MASSIVE TRAUMA

Irma Grese was born in 1923 in Germany. In 1936 her mother committed suicide. I believe Grese then found some sort of structure or mentoring within the League of German Girls (Bund Deutscher Mädel), the branch of Hitler Youth for girls. It also appears she took high-ranking Nazi lovers at Auschwitz and climbed the ladder to the top. Eventually, she was able to become an SS guard. Grese's father had told her that working for the Nazis was a horrible way to develop a career for herself. When she wouldn't listen to her father's advice, he disowned her. Though I'd spent years exploring the psychology of Nazi killers, the following information was unknown to me before I had traveled to the camps.

Grese had control of over thirty thousand Jewish women and decided who would live and who would die. She selected which women would enter the gas chambers. She was a vicious creature who shot, hanged, tortured, humiliated, and killed women by any means. In the camps this extremely over-empowered woman was tried for war crimes at the age of twenty-two and then hanged by the neck. Adding up the dates I strongly suspect my husband's aunt and other women who were friends of the family came to a crossroads with Irma Grese.

As I said previously, for me walking through the Nazi death camps was gut wrenching. The murky energy of the place made it extremely difficult to be there. I couldn't begin to imagine what those who had been tormented and murdered within these walls had actually gone through. Auschwitz with its massive tragedies, violent deaths, and abuses was beyond my comprehension. Walking through the remaining ashes of so many victims, in a building built with pure evil, left me feeling sick and grief stricken.

This journey showed me why my in-laws, my husband's aunt, and members of my family had behaved the way they did. It was never about me. It was about their history and tragedies. When we went into one of the gas chambers that had been bombed by the allies, I suddenly felt so sick I could hardly stand up. Generally, it didn't smell in the camp, but at certain locations there were very unpleasant odors. The devastation of these places is still holding on.

The saving grace for such gruesome events has been the accounts of acts of courage the camp victims displayed to save families, friends, fellow prisoners, and themselves. These brave men and women, young and old, from all walks of life, have helped me accept an undeniable truth. Regardless of this history of hate, there truly are angels among us.

THE SPIRITUAL CORE OF JUDAISM

Before I started looking into afterlife research and Jewish mysticism or began examining the spiritual experiences documented within Jewish history and outside Judaism, I'd become very disillusioned with the Jewish religion. Everything began to feel like a sales pitch. The constant commercials from the pulpit and with newsletters requesting money wore me out and buried the true beauty of the religion. It appeared to me that too many of those who were in control were going to do whatever was necessary to remain there for power, prestige, politics, or dominance.

I know others who have become disillusioned. Some friends of mine have developed an almost secularized form of Judaism, which at times can feel antiseptic. A noticeable number of individuals are running away from Judaism and moving toward all sorts of other paths such as Buddhism, New Age paths, other religions, agnostic ways of thinking, and even atheism. I, myself, checked out all these philosophies, and though I continue to have an appetite for spiritual answers and direction outside Judaism, much of this has been a disappointing quest.

When I've asked those lapsed Jews I've known what concerns them about Judaism, a few of the responses have been:

I don't believe in religion. I always feel like a subordinate.

It feels like pablum for the masses.

I like my partner's religion better than mine.

When I was sick, it wasn't my rabbi who called or came over to help. It was friends and neighbors who showed up.

All I ever get are notes about dues.

I'm new and very shy, and it's hard to go up to a congregant and introduce myself.

Only certain congregants are seen as important.

I experienced abuse at a temple when I was a child, but no one would believe me.

The sense of exclusion really got to me.

If I go to services, I feel freighted by what's being read at the pulpit.

When I've needed guidance, the rabbi is never anywhere to be found or he's too busy.

I get nothing out of it.

Where is God? I prayed and prayed and was still in so much pain.

When I was going through a divorce, I went to a rabbi, and all he did was give me pages to read.

My parents have great financial security, so the Temple expects me to pay high dues, even though I'm raising four boys and two girls.

Many synagogue activities were out of my price range.

I find that because I'm a new congregant, I'm expected to do too much volunteer work.

Some of it feels so fake.

I finally discovered another activity or group where I can make a link with my spiritual self.

After I had a powerful spiritual experience elsewhere, I began to pull away from Judaism.

Despite my disillusionment with Judaism, I couldn't help being aware of how people from temple took care of me while I was so very sick with cancer. A couple showed up at our doorstep with homemade soup, bread, baked chicken, and an assortment of yummy desserts. Several congregants sent cards, and a leader in the temple called to see if I was all right. Know that I'm not suggesting the religion is losing itself into some black hole. Rather, my question is: Are all the spiritual needs in the world family of Judaism truly being included? In my explorations of the spiritual aspect of Judaism, understand I'm not talking about just rabbis, leaders, temples, and synagogues or different divisions of the religion.

For me personally, Judaism and spirituality have always gone together. I can't imagine one without the other. Today when I go to temple or synagogue on Shabbat and recite holy prayers, I know Jews around the world are doing the same. During these times, I connect with a part of history. I can find peace in nature, the high mountains, vast seas, and my own backyard and with meditation. Writing, art, music, woodwork, and watching children or pets play are just a few activities that can help me unite with my divine self. This is a source of spirituality, the shard of a gem from an unknown place or Ein Sof. During such times I feel connected with all living beings. I have seen the web of life. The bond is strong, and these spiritual experiences bring hope.

The Journey Continues

Across the ages, from centuries ago to modern times, freethinkers have taken risks by sharing their narratives about what they saw or experienced during an afterlife contact. Do we have to believe in another religion or philosophy to accept an afterlife? Are we ready to open and talk about how the fear of death blunts our spiritual evolution? The voyage will not end with physical death. As we reexamine old ideas that no longer suit our spiritual needs, know that we can always return to them if we feel like it.

Our journey has ended. It's time we part ways and move along our separate paths. My hope is, you have gathered a few pearls to take with you. These will help you to develop and lay a foundation with some of your ideas, religious beliefs, and spiritual interests. I'm feeling very optimistic that you have received information that resonates with your spirit and personal sense of spirituality. There is an old saying that goes something like: "Take what works for you and leave the rest on a shelf." Maybe it isn't time for you to look at changing paths and not all the pages in this book may be your cup of tea—and that's just fine. Recognize this early groundwork is only meant to be a new starting point on your trek.

APPENDIX

~A~ Self-Awareness Inventory
Reviewing Your Own Life Book

*Whoever is able to write a book, and does not, it is as if he
has lost a child.*

—RABBI NACHMAN OF BRESLOV

It's now time for you to look through the pages in your life book.
Because we are the recipients and inheritors of generations of trauma,
we must take responsibility and try to sort this out. Just answer a few
questions or prompts per day. There are no timekeepers; nobody is
watching. Know you cannot flunk this inventory: I promise.

The Early Years: Childhood through Adolescence

Religion

> Do you think you had a normal religious upbringing? How was it
> normal?
>
> Have you ever been made to fear religion?
>
> Do you believe you received healthy religious direction when you
> were growing up?

How was your childhood rabbi?

What rabbi or teacher made the biggest impact upon you?

Which clergy did you like the most? Rabbis, teachers, or youth counselors?

Which clergy did you like the least? Rabbis, teachers, or youth counselors?

Were you ever yelled at, shamed, or intimidated by clergy? Do you feel the response by clergy was not fair, too extreme, demeaning, or shaming?

If you did get into trouble for acting inappropriately in Hebrew class or Sunday school, do you think you received a proper response from teachers and rabbis?

What's the best thing you remember about going to temple or synagogue? Spend a few minutes thinking about this. Write a few lines about a temple event that left you with great memories.

What's the worst thing you remember about going to temple or synagogue? Spend a few minutes thinking about this.

Did you have a group from Sunday school or Hebrew school to goof around with?

What Jewish organizations or camp groups did you enjoy?

If you didn't enjoy religious groups, why?

Were either of your parents involved with temple or synagogue?

If so, did their position within the Jewish community make you agitated, annoyed, proud, or did you not pay attention?

Were you teased for being Jewish?

Dating and Food

Did you only date those within the Jewish community?

If you dated outside the Jewish religion, how did your parents react?

What Judaic food did you like?

Do you eat Jewish, German, Czechoslovakian, Hungarian, Israeli, Russian, Polish, Ashkenazi, or Eastern European food?

Did you or do you now eat these foods only at home, synagogue, or Jewish functions?

Do you enjoy the religious aspect of consuming this food?

Emotions: Childhood to Adulthood

Anger

Have you ever been punished for breaking the no-talk rule, telling secrets, expressing emotion, having an opinion, crying, or getting angry or had an adult tell you: "If you can't say something nice, don't say anything at all." "If you're angry, just get busy and find something constructive to do." I have worked with several individuals who unknowingly carry their caregivers' baggage.

Did your parents allow you to be angry? Was it safe to be angry around your parents? What did they do or say to you when you were angry?

What did your father do when he got angry? How did you feel about his anger?

What did your mother do when she got angry? How did you feel about her anger?

What did you do when either of your parents were angry?

Did you witness your parents yelling, being sarcastic, screaming, slamming doors, throwing dishes, vases, or food on the floor, or using derogatory terms? List what you witnessed and reflect for a few moments on how this made you feel.

Was there physical abuse between your parents? Did you witness pushing, shoving, and hitting? If you witnessed this, it's called witness abuse.

Many of those I've worked with have said their parents never got angry. If your parents didn't rage openly at each other or you, how else did they express this emotion? Did you witness silent rage (feeling a person is angry without verbalizing it)? Expressions of silent rage include workaholism, food addictions, silent anger toward God, refusing to express any emotion, controlling money, being dishonest, privately self-destructing, withholding love or compliments, not taking care of the physical body, purposefully hurting the physical body such as by cutting. See if you can relate to any of this: make a list of how you witnessed silent rage and reflect for a few moments on how it made you feel. Children cannot feel safe if their parents or caretakers are verbally or silently raging.

Anger can be a form of depression. How do you feel about this statement?

How did you know when your parents were just disagreeing with each other and not raging? Not learning how to have healthy anger stunts our development when it comes to healthy confrontational skills. Who of us wants to be a doormat or pushover? What do you think about the previous statements?

In a healthy relationship people respect one another's boundaries. At the same time, we can still disagree with one another. What do these statements mean to you?

Do you see any similarities between your wife, husband, or significant other and your mother, father, or primary caretaker in relation to how anger was dealt with while you were growing up?

Do you express your anger like your mother or father?

Is it safe to be angry around your wife, husband, or significant other?

As an adult can you tell your parents when you are angry?

Sadness

Was crying okay in your family or did you cry only when you were alone?

Were you ever punished for crying?

When you are depressed or sad, what do you do or who do you talk to about this?

What did your father do when he was sad or depressed?

What did your mother do when she was sad or depressed?

What does your significant other do when sad or depressed?

Do you see any similarities between your mother, father, significant other, and you?

Guilt, Shame

Could you distinguish between guilt and shame when younger? As an adult? Shame means: "I'm no good! I'm despicable." Guilt means: "I did something wrong and I will make amends and restitution for this and not do it again." Does the above make sense to you?

Were you told as a young child that God would punish you for your behavior?

If you explored yourself sexually as a child or adolescent, were you called a sinner or ungodly?

Using God as a means of punishment is spiritually abusive and leaves us with an angry, frightening, untrustworthy, hurtful perception of a higher power or God. Did you know this?

Feelings toward and about Parents

Do you protect your parents?

Do you believe there is nothing your mother wouldn't do for you?

Would your father do anything for you?

Do you think your parents did or do love each other?

Emotional, Physical, Spiritual, or Sexual Abuse

Physical abuse is a dysfunctional expression of anger. If we do not face our true feelings about this, we are very at risk for inflicting physical or emotional abuse on others. Emotional abuse can damage for a lifetime.

Sexual abuse not only causes long-lasting scars but also self-destructive tendencies.

> List examples of ways in which you may have experienced: emotional, physical, spiritual, or sexual abuse.
>
> Have you ever been physically abused by anyone? Slapped, punched, pushed, or hit with a belt, coat hanger, or hairbrush?
>
> Think of an incident where the actions of a family member (mother, father, sibling, or cousin) or caretaker (neighbor, religious leader, babysitter, or teacher) left you feeling extremely depressed, self-destructive, angry, or numb. Or think of a time when you felt betrayed by a significant person in your life (mother, father, sibling, teacher, etc.). Write a few lines about this.
>
> Were you ever touched inappropriately physically or sexually by a rabbi, Sunday schoolteacher, counselor, or synagogue staff? Did you try to talk with someone about this, but were dismissed, or shamed?
>
> After abusive experiences did you find yourself pulling away from God and religious organizations?
>
> Is there any sort of touch from anyone that left you feeling uncomfortable? Have you ever felt like an embrace or hug was too tight? Have you talked to someone about this?
>
> Were you sexually abused, such as being inappropriately touched or being made to touch an older child or adult?

Family History: The Holocaust

> Did any of your parents, grandparents, or other extended family live through or die during the Holocaust?
>
> Take a moment to list the names of anyone in your family, extended family, friends, teachers, their children who survived or died during the Holocaust or were the offspring of Holocaust survivors?

Despair, Suicide, Death, Grief

Have you ever felt suicidal? If yes, who have you talked to about this?

Have you had little or no hope? Can you explain why?

Has anyone ever said to you, "Well, I survived or lost family during the Holocaust, so wipe your eyes and pull yourself together!"

Has your mother or father passed away? If so, how old were you and how did you react or feel?

Have you ever experienced the death of someone special? How did you react? Did you feel numb (numb is a feeling), frightened, rageful, regretful, extremely distressed, or panicked? Did you start drinking or using medication more often?

Have you become angry at God for the loss of someone close?

Did you cry or talk to someone, a therapist or safe clergy person, about this loss? If not, can you take a few moments to think why you may have "stuffed" your feelings about this loss?

Are you aware that unexpressed grief can present with extreme emotion, not expressing difficult feelings, and mistrust in any type of higher power, with self-destructive behavior, or rage? Think about this for a few moments and write about it.

From Darkness to Light: Experiencing God and Religion as an Adult

Do you still go to temple or a synagogue? Do you enjoy it?

Have you changed to another religion? If so, why?

Do you feel like God or some higher power is guiding you?

If you could create your own idea of a god, from appearances to personality, what would this look like?

Issues with the current god of our understanding can keep us at odds with a healthy form of spirituality. Compare the god of your youth with a god you would like to have. What did you discover? Remember there are no wrong answers.

Do you mistrust:
- Any form of a god
- Higher power
- Creative force
- Life force
- Psychic energy
- Guiding intelligence
- Quantum mechanics
- Spiritual understanding
- Science
- Order and determination of nature
- Belief in an afterlife
- Certainty we are not the only living creatures in this universe
- Certainty we are the only living creatures in this universe

ARGUING WITH GOD

In the famous play *Fiddler on the Roof* one of the main characters is Tevye, a Jewish dairy man living in a village in the Pale settlement of Imperial Russia. It was never a dull existence in the village. Because of scarcity of food, famine, and sickness, life for the families could quickly turn for the worst. In the early 1900s, Tevye with his five daughters and wife began to watch their simple survival slipping away. Abuses and political demonstrations left this father, his family, and other villagers feeling the increasing unrest moving closer and closer to them. Their rights, lands, homes, livestock, way of being, and religion were being taken from them. Eventually, a Russian constable tells all the village dwellers to pick up their belongings and leave their homes within three days.

Throughout the play, Tevye talks, argues, and laments to God about his wife, daughters, their husbands, and how difficult living as a Jew in Russia has become. Anti-Semitism is on the rise, and Tevye has lots to say about this during his ongoing debates with God. One of my favorite quotes in the play is when Tevye argues with God by saying, "It may sound like I am complaining, but not a lot. After all, with your help, I'm starving to death."

Based on my experiences and investigations, Jews have been arguing and yelling at God for centuries. Cursing at God also happens. If you think about it, this is a relief. When we are upset, distressed, angry, grief stricken, or frightened, we can "have words" with the god of our understanding. So, is it okay for you to honestly talk and even argue with God?

Developing healthy spirituality can take some time. This is not something that will happen overnight. As a matter of fact, we will need to go through a process of trial and error. A lot of individuals will visit different religious organizations to see what they are like. Then they will discover this is not what they want in their spiritual life. I suggest sitting in the back of the room of the temple or synagogue. I still do that to this day. Having a touch of open-mindedness is a must. Always remember that we can move on to another spiritual institution if we want to.

Bob Dylan would come into a synagogue with his prayer shawl covering his entire head and upper body. Sitting or standing at the rear end of the sanctuary, he would just listen. With his prayer shawl he wouldn't be recognized. By doing this I bet he was able to continue working on his own concept of spirituality in private. He most likely studied several branches of Judaism, and I bet you he also looked at some other sects of organized spirituality.

If your place of worship doesn't feel comfortable for you, move on to a new experience but take it slowly. You don't have to commit; you don't have to donate money. You don't have to talk to anybody unless you want to, but understand that you can always ask questions.

All of us have some innate inner feeling about spirituality. While I was searching, I went to several different synagogues, mosques, churches, and other religious organizations. Honestly, I didn't know what to believe and had to weed out what sort of spirituality worked for me.

Everything felt so confusing, so for a few years my sanctuary was the mountains, sitting on a gigantic rock, and looking at lower Boulder and Denver. The tears I would shed were spiritual. I felt the presence of some sort of intelligence and enlightenment.

When we stopped going to Boulder, I would walk the trails of the Blue Ridge Mountains in North Carolina. Sometimes my family and I would drive up a road and look over ledges and cliffs at the magnificent mountains. This experience was a spiritual experience. I love hiking and seeing what I can see. Each time I've gone up into the mountains or spent time with the ocean, I've felt this overwhelming sense of the presence of something much greater than myself.

I also made the trek to England, Ireland, Czech Republic, Hungry, Belarus, Poland, Germany, Scotland, and parts of Eastern and Western Europe. Along the way I've met some very interesting people. There were individuals with different spiritual beliefs, speaking all sorts of languages. Those who were too overly involved with religion or certain philosophies also taught me many lessons. I knew in my soul that any religious belief lived in the extreme was not healthy or balanced. Wanting to live an aware and conscious life, with tools that would help me navigate my journey, was a must.

After several years, I'm finally very comfortable with my own sense of spirituality. Will this last? Probably not. In time and down the road, I will most likely be removing while adding a few things to my spiritual toolbox. That said, I will be keeping those ideas and experiences that continue to fit my spirit. Trying to figure out what type of spiritual being we can be is painful but rewarding. As a Jew I found many things within certain parts of the religion that just didn't fit for me. Letting go without feeling shame was a difficult task. I would feel this nagging sense of guilt and even shame in the back of my brain telling me I must continue to do this to be a good Jew. With this mentality I felt trapped and said to myself, "You really are a bad Jew." This attitude kept me stuck, and there was no way I could make movement toward appreciating Judaism. Along with this my authentic self was pushed back into the closet, and the door was nailed shut.

All of us are individual freethinkers. About our spirituality, what works for you may not work for me.

Several years ago, I had an incredible dream about my mother. In this dream I saw myself hiking up a mountain covered with beautiful flowers. I went up to the top of the peak to meet with my mother in spirit. Looking down into the valley, I sensed each flower had its own inner sense of self. Every single flower was a different color. Yes, they were all flowers but each was a different color—pink, green, blue, yellow, orange, purple, turquoise, magenta, and a host of other majestic colors I had never seen before in my life. Though we are still flowers, it's the colorful blossoms that define us. This individuality makes the whole mountain a beautiful, very exciting, and interesting place to visit.

This is how I like to describe our spiritual bond with one another. As I said, we are all different colored flowers, but our mutual characteristics, the leaves, stems, and branches, provide us with a sense of unity and hope.

> *The pursuit of knowledge for its own sake, an almost fanatical love of justice and the desire for personal independence—these are the features of the Jewish tradition which make me thank my stars that I belong to it.*
>
> —ALBERT EINSTEIN

> *Even through grief, physical struggles, and sorrow, always trust good things are still possible.*
>
> —CARLA WILLS-BRANDON

Know that just by reading the words in the above chapters you have given me a very precious gift. Please don't forget to care for yourself and peek at the inventory.

I wish you the very best, as you continue exploring your own special sense of spirituality.

References

Alexander, Eben, and Ptolemy Tompkins. *The Map of Heaven: How Science, Religion, and Ordinary People Are Proving the Afterlife*. New York: Simon and Schuster, 2014.

Anthony, Mark, and Gary Schwartz. *The Afterlife Frequency: The Scientific Proof of Spiritual Contact and How That Awareness Will Change Your Life*. Novato, Calif.: New World Library, 2021.

Aries, Philippe. *The Hour of Our Death: The Classic History of Western Attitudes Toward Death over the Last One Thousand Years*. 2nd ed. New York: Knopf, 1981.

Astor, Yaakov. *Soul Searching: Seeking Scientific Ground for the Jewish Tradition of an Afterlife*. Southfield, Mich.: Targum Press, 2003.

Barak, Yoram, Dov Aizenberg, Henry Szor, Marnina Swartz, Rachel Maor, and Haim Y. Knobler. "Increased Risk of Attempted Suicide among Aging Holocaust Survivors." *American Journal of Geriatric Psychiatry* 13, no. 8 (August 2005): 701–4.

Barrett, Sir William. *Deathbed Visions*. Guildford, UK: White Crow Books, 2011.

Bevers, Sabine. "10 Interesting Cases of Supposed Reincarnation." Listverse, October 21, 2013.

Blech, Benjamin. *Hope, Not Fear: Changing the Way We View Death*. Lanham, Md.: Rowman and Little, 2018.

Blumenthal, Ralph. "An Ever-Curious Spirit, Unbeaten after 111 Years." *New York Times*, May 4, 2014.

Brodsky-Chenfeld, Dan. *Above All Else: A World Champion Skydiver's Story of*

Survival and What It Taught Him about Fear, Adversity, and Success. New York: Skyhorse, 2011.

Buber, Martin. *Tales of the Hasidim: The Early Masters.* Vol. 2. 1st ed. New York: Schocken Books, 2022.

Burke, George. *May a Christian Believe in Reincarnation?* 2nd ed. Cedar Crest, N.M.: Light of the Spirit Press, 2014.

Carlyle, Thomas. "The Hero as Prophet." In *On Heroes, Hero-Worship and the Heroic in History,* 44. Lincoln: University of Nebraska Press, 1966. First published 1841.

Chapman, Fern Schumer. *Motherland: Beyond the Holocaust; A Mother-Daughter Journey to Reclaim the Past.* New York: Penguin Books, 2001.

Chris. "Are There Ghosts in Auschwitz?" Real Paranormal Experiences, June 24, 2021.

Cohen, Abraham. *Everyman's Talmud: The Major Teachings of the Rabbinic Sages.* New York: J. M. Dent, 1934.

Cohen, Zamir. "The Near-Death Experience of Sharon Nachshoni." My Western Wall, October 13, 2013.

Currin, Grayson H. "Bob Dylan: Time Out of Mind." Pitchfork, May 13, 2018.

Demitrius. "Orbs: The Souls of the Dead?" Ocprstoronto, November 18, 2012.

Dubov, Nissan D. "The Soul and the Afterlife." Chabad.org.

Einstein, Albert. *The World As I See It.* Minneapolis, Minn.: Filiquarian, 2006. First published 1934.

Epstein, Nadine, and Rebecca Frankel. "Bob Dylan: The Unauthorized Spiritual Biography." *Moment Magazine,* July 2005.

Fahmy, Dalia. "Key Findings about Americans' Belief in God." Pew Research Center, April 25, 2018.

Feinstein, Tikvah. *Music from a Broken Violin: A Memoir.* Ambridge, Penn.: Taproot Press, 2011.

Fenwick, Peter. *Shining Light on Transcendence: The Unconventional Journey of a Neuroscientist.* Guildford, UK: White Crow Books, 2019.

Fox, Glenn R., Jonas Kaplan, Hanna Damasio, and Antonio Damasio. "Neural Correlates of Gratitude." *Frontiers in Psychology* 6 (September 30, 2015).

Freyberger, Harald J., and Hellmuth Freyberger. "60 Years Later: Posttraumatic Stress Disorders, Salutogenic Factors and Medical Expert Assessment in Holocaust Survivors in the Long-Term Course." *Zeitschrift für Psychosomatische Medizin und Psychotherapie* 53, no. 4 (2007): 380–92.

Gabrielsen, F., "After Lenin, Soviet Anti-Semitism Grew." *New York Times,* February 20, 1990.

Gettleman, Jeffrey, and Isabel Kershner. "Benjamin Netanyahu Traces Path to Power Back to Entebbe, and Lost Brother." *New York Times,* July 4, 2016.

Gilbert, Barbara. *From Ashes to the Rainbow: A Tribute to Raoul Wallenberg; Works by Alice Lok Cahana.* Los Angeles: Hebrew Union College Skirball Museum, 1986.

Goldberg, Michael. "Audio: Bob Dylan Attends Buddy Holly Show—January 31, 1959" (blog). Days of the Crazy—Wild, January 31, 2014.

Greyson, Bruce. *Afterlife: A Doctor Explores What Near-Death Experiences Reveal about Life and Beyond.* New York: St. Martin's Essentials, 2021.

———. "Is Consciousness Produced by the Brain?" YouTube video, 1:24:06. Cosmology and Consciousness, third conference. Tibetan Children's Villages Auditorium. Dharamasala, Northern India: Library of Tibetan Works and Archives, 2011.

Guibbory, Moses. *The Bible in the Hands of its Creators: Biblical Facts as They Are.* Translated by David Horowitz. English and Hebrew ed. Jerusalem, New York: Society of the Bible in the Hands of its Creators, 1943.

Hadler, Jeffrey. "Translations of Antisemitism: Jews, the Chinese, and Violence in Colonial and Post-Colonial Indonesia." *Indonesia and the Malay World* 32, no. 94 (January 1, 2004): 291.

Head, Joseph, and S. L. Cranston, eds. *Reincarnation: A Living Study of Reincarnation in All Ages.* New York: Causeway Books, 1967.

HaLevi, Baruch. "Do Jews Believe in Hell?" JewishBoston, June 18, 2013.

Haraldsson, Erlendur. *The Departed Among the Living: An Investigative Study of Afterlife Encounters.* Guildford, UK: White Crow Books, 2012.

Haraldsson, Erlendur, and Osis Karlis. *At the Hour of Death: A New Look at Evidence for Life after Death.* Guildford, UK: White Crow Books, 2012.

Imich, Alexander, ed. *Incredible Tales of the Paranormal: Documented Accounts of Poltergeist, Levitations, Phantoms, and Other Phenomena.* New York: Bramble Books, 1995.

Holden, Janice Miner, Bruce Greyson, and Debbie James, eds. *The Handbook of Near-Death Experiences: Thirty Years of Investigation.* Santa Barbara, Calif.: Praeger, 2009.

Huberman, Jack. *The Quotable Atheist: Ammunition for Non-Believers, Political Junkies, Gadflies, and Those Generally Hell-Bound.* New York: Nation Books, 2007.

Hummel, Virginia. *Orbs and the Afterlife: Survival of the Soul.* Independently published, 2017.

Jacobs, Louis, ed. *The Jewish Religion: A Companion.* Oxford, UK: Oxford University Press, 1995.

Jacobsen, Thorkild. "Mesopotamian Religion." *Encyclopaedia Britannica,* July 26, 1999.

James, William. *The Varieties of Religious Experience: A Study of Human Nature.* 3rd ed. New York: Collier Books, 1961.

Jewish Virtual Library. "Bob Dylan (1941–)." Biography, n.d.

———. "Joseph Stalin (1879–1953)." Biography, under "Hannah Arendt," n.d.

———. "Rabbi Yisrael Baal Shem Tov (1698–1760)." Biography, n.d.

Jewison, Norman, dir. *Fiddler on the Roof.* Screenplay by Joseph Stein. 3 hrs. Beverly Hills, Calif.: Metro Goldwyn Mayer, 1971. Internet Archive.

JPost.com staff. "Netanyahu Visits Gravesite of Brother Yoni on Anniversary of Entebbe Raid." *Jerusalem Post,* July 4, 2014.

Judaism 101. "Olam Ha-Ba: The Afterlife." JewFAQ.

Kirsta, Alix. "The Trauma of Second-Generation Holocaust Survivors." *Guardian,* March 17, 2014.

Klein, Tienke. "Tienke Klein NDE—Nazi Concentration Camp Survivor Near Death Experience." NDE Video. YouTube video, 9:36, n.d.

Kübler-Ross, Elisabeth. *The Tunnel and the Light: Essential Insights on Living and Dying.* Scottsdale, Ariz.: Elisabeth Kübler-Ross Family Limited Partnership, 1999.

Kutch, K., and B. J. Cox. "Symptoms of PTSD in 124 Survivors of the Holocaust." *American Journal of Psychiatry* 149, no. 3 (March 1992): 337–40.

LaRoe, Diane. *The Awakening.* Bloomington, Ind.: Authorhouse, 2005. First published 1999.

———. "Personal correspondence," interview by Carla Wills-Brandon. Bloomington, Ind.: Authorhouse, 2005.

Leider, Susan. "When Moses Boils Over, We Take Stock of Our Own Anger." *Jewish News of Northern California,* June 29, 2017.

Leiter, Shaul Yosef. "The Soul of Man Is the Candle of G-d." Chabad.org, 2003.

Lewak, Doree. "My Dad Howard Stern Put Me off Dating Men." *New York Post,* November 8, 2015.

Lewis, Mark. "Religion and Addiction: Void-Fillers?: Losing One's Faith Can Feel like Facing Everlasting Abstinence." *Psychology Today,* May 26, 2015.

Litvak, Salvador. "I Saw My Grandmother's Soul Leave Her Body." *Hevria* magazine, 2015.

Long, Jeffrey, and Paul Perry. *Evidence of the Afterlife: The Science of Near-Death Experiences.* New York: HarperOne, 2009.

Lowers, Elise, and Julene Anderson. *Orbs: The Untold Story.* Bloomington, Ind.: Balboa Press, 2013.

Macintyre, Donald. "Binyamin Netanyahu Visits Scene of Brother's 1976 Entebbe Airport Death." *Guardian,* July 4, 2017.

Mark, Jonathan. "The Other Side Of Dying." NY Jewish Week, December 31, 2018.

Mason, Richard. *The God of Spinoza: A Philosophical Study.* Cambridge, UK: Cambridge University Press, 1999.

Mead, Wendy. "The Day the Music Died: Rock's Great Tragedy." Biography.com, February 1, 2019.

Medzini, Meron. *Under the Shadow of the Rising Sun: Japan and the Jews during the Holocaust Era.* Boston: Academic Studies Press, 2019.

Mishpacha. "Judaism and Death." Mishpacha.org, Memorial Foundation for Jewish Culture, n.d.

Moody, Raymond. *Life After Life: The Bestselling Original Investigation That Revealed "Near-Death Experiences."* 2nd ed. New York: HarperOne, 2015. First published 1975.

Morin, Richard. "Do Americans Believe in God?" *Washington Post,* April 24, 2000.

Murphy, Caryle. "Most Americans Believe in Heaven . . . and Hell." Pew Research Center, November 10, 2015.

Netanyahu, Benjamin. "'OBJECTified': One-on-One with Benjamin Netanyahu." Interview by Harvey Levin. Fox News, October 6, 2017.

Neumann, Jonathan. "Near-Death Experiences in Judaic Literature." *Journal of Psychology and Judaism* 14, no. 4 (Winter 1990).

Noam, Rachel. *The View from Above.* Lakewood, N.J.: C.I.S., 1992.

O'Neal, Sam. "What's the Difference Between Pharisees and Sadducees?" Learn Religions, June 25, 2019.

OU staff. "Hasidic Wisdom." *Orthodox Union,* February 11, 2014.

Pew, Alan. "The Significance of the Near-Death Experience in Western Cultural Traditions." Master's thesis, California State University, 1999.

Pew Research Center. "The Pew Research Center's Forum on Religion & Public Life to Release New Poll on Changes in Religious Affiliation in the U.S." *PRC Forum,* April 20, 2009.

———. "The Religious Typology." *PRC Report,* August 29, 2018.

Pinkham, Mark A. "The Origin of the Knights Templar—Descendants of Jewish Elders?" *Ancient Origins: Reconstructing the Story of Humanity's Past,* February 10, 2021.

Quinn, Rob. "Oldest Man, 111, Spent Last Hours Talking to Spirits." Newser, June 9, 2014.

Ratzabi, Hila. "The Zohar." My Jewish Learning, n.d.

Read, C. *Lenin: A Revolutionary Life.* New York: Routledge, 2005.

Resnick, Benjamin. "What Judaism Says about Reincarnation." My Jewish Learning, n.d.

Ricci, Ronit. "Introduction: Jews in Indonesia: Perceptions and Histories." *Indonesia and the Malay World* 38, no. 112 (November 2010): 325–27.

Rigler, Sara Yoheved. "Life After Death." Aish.com, n.d.

———. "Reincarnation and the Holocaust." Aish.com, n.d.

Ring, Kenneth. *Life at Death.* New York: William Morrow, 1982.

Ritchie, George G., and Elizabeth Sherrill. *Return from Tomorrow.* Minneapolis, Minn.: Chosen, 2007. First published 1978.

Ritchie, Jean. *Death's Door: True Stories of Near Death Experiences.* London: Michael O'Mara Books, 1994.

Rivas, Titus, Anny Dirven, and Rudolf H. Smit. *The Self Does Not Die: Verified Paranormal Phenomena from Near-Death Experiences.* Durham, N.C.: IANDS, 2016.

Ross, Allen P. *Introducing Biblical Hebrew.* Ada, Mich.: Baker Academic, 2001.

Ross, Lesli Koppelman. "Yom Hashoah: What Does It Mean?—Religious Importance." In *Celebrate: The Complete Jewish Holidays Handbook,* 60–61. New York: Jason Aronson Book/Rowman and Littlefield, 1994.

Ryan, Thomas. "25 Percent of US Christians Believe in Reincarnation. What's Wrong with This Picture?" *America* magazine, October 21, 2015.

Sabom, Michael B. *Recollections of Death: A Medical Investigation.* New York: HarperCollins, 1982.

Seligson, Dan. "Bob Dylan's Long-Lost Israel Song." JewishBoston, January 8, 2018.

Schiller, Ferdinand C. S. *Humanism: Philosophical Essays.* Westport, Conn.: Greenwood Press, 1970. First published 1912.

———. *Must Philosophers Disagree and Other Essays in Popular Philosophy.* London: Macmillan, 1934.

Schniedewind, William M. "Prolegomena for the Sociolinguistics of Classical Hebrew." *Journal of Hebrew Scriptures* 5 (December 31, 2005).

Shiyovich, Arthur, Ygal Plakht, Katya Belinski, and Harel Gilutz. "Characteristics and Long-Term Prognosis of Holocaust Survivors Presenting with Acute Myocardial Infarction." *Israel Medical Association Journal* 18, no. 5 (April 30, 2016): 252–56.

Spinoza, Benedictus De. *The Ethics of Spinoza: The Road to Inner Freedom.* Edited by Dagobert D. Runes. New York: Citadel Press, 1957.

———.*Improvement of the Understanding, Ethics, and Correspondence of Benedict De Spinoza.* Translated by R. H. M. Elwes. Introduction by Frank Sewall. Whitefish, Mont.: Kessinger, 2010. First published 1901.

Steiger, Brad, and John White. *Other Worlds, Other Universes: Playing the Reality Game.* Guildford, UK: White Crow Books, 2020.

Stevenson, Ian. *European Cases of the Reincarnation Type.* New York: Macmillan, 2008.

Stern, Howard. "Stern Family Memories . . . of Death & Depression." Howard Stern website, February 27, 2013.

Student, Rabbi Gil. "What Is the Jewish View on Ghosts?" Orthodox Union, July 20, 2016.

Swift, Mary. "Howard Stern: 'Meditation Is Just like Brushing Your Teeth!'" Transcendental Meditation, November 16, 2013.

Tibon, Amir, and Ben Birnbaum. "'Is This Ship Sinking?' Inside the Collapse of the Campaign Against Netanyahu." *New Yorker,* March 20, 2015.

Tilles, Yerachmiel. "Judaism and Reincarnation: Kabbalah on Judaism and Reincarnation." Chabad.org, n.d.

Traubmann, Tamara. "Study: Holocaust Survivors 3 Times More Likely to Attempt Suicide." *Haaretz,* August 9, 2005.

Turner, René Hope. "Rene Hope Turner NDE: Experience Description." Near-Death Experience Research Foundation, February 24, 1982.

Tymn, Michael. "Dr. Peter Fenwick Discusses Dying, Death and Survival." Michael Tymn's blog. White Crow Books, May 27, 2012.

———. "109-Year-Old Scientist Continues to Pursue Illumination." Michael Tymn's blog. White Crow Books, February 3, 2012.

United Israel Bulletin. "David Horowitz: A Life Remembered (1902–2002)." *United Israel Bulletin* 61, no. 1 (December 2015): 6–8.

U.S. Department of Veterans Affairs. "Sexual Assault: Children." National Center for PTSD, n.d.

U.S. Holocaust Memorial Museum. "Who Were the Victims?" Holocaust Encyclopedia, March 4, 2020.

van Lommel, Pim. *Consciousness Beyond Life: The Science of the Near-Death Experience*. New York: HarperOne, 2011. First published 2007 as *Eindeloos Bewustzijn*.

Wehrstein, K. M. "Past Life Memories of the Holocaust." *Psi Encyclopedia,* November 7, 2017.

White, John. "Resurrection and the Body of Light." *Quest* 97, no. 1 (Fall 2009): 11–15.

Wiesel, Elie. "Living with an Open Heart." Interview by Oprah Winfrey. *Super Soul Sunday,* December 9, 2012. YouTube video.

———. *Night*. New York: Bantam Books, 1982.

Williams, Kevin. "Dr. Rene Turner's Near-Death Experience." *Near-Death Experiences and the Afterlife,* September 27, 2019.

———. *Nothing Better Than Death: Insights from Sixty-Two Profound Near-Death Experiences*. Independently published, 2019.

———. "Reincarnation in Early Christianity." *Near-Death Experiences and the Afterlife,* September 27, 2019.

Wills-Brandon, Carla. *A Glimpse of Heaven: The Remarkable World of Spiritually Transformative Experiences*. Guildford, UK: White Crow Books, 2012.

———. *Heavenly Hugs: Comfort, Support, and Hope from the Afterlife*. Pompton Plains, N.J.: New Page Books, 2012.

———. *Learning to Say No: Establishing Healthy Boundaries*. Deerfield Beach, Fla.: HCI Books, 2000.

———. "Looking Deeper into the Myth That Progressive Jews Don't Believe in an Afterlife." Carla Wills-Brandon's blog. White Crow Books, November 17, 2014.

———. *One Last Hug before I Go: The Mystery and Meaning of Deathbed Visions.* Deerfield Beach, Fla.: HCI Books, 2010.

Winston, Pinchas. *Fundamentals of Reincarnation: A Course about the Fundamentals of Reincarnation Based upon Sha'ar HaGilgulim from the Arizal.* Independently published, 2017.

Woods, Don E. "Vineland's Raab Family Continues Legacy of Education about the Holocaust." NJ.com: True Jersey, January 28, 2013.

Yamamoto, Mayumi. "Spell of the Rebel, Monumental Apprehensions: Japanese Discourses on Pieter Erberveld." *Indonesia,* no. 77 (2004): 109–43.

Yanklowitz, Shmuly. "Reborn Again? A Jewish Moral Argument for Reincarnation." NY Jewish Week, June 11, 2010.

Yeshshem. "Basic Class 11—Reincarnation." Reincarnation in Judaism, n.d.

Zammit, Victor, and Wendy Zammit. *A Lawyer Presents the Evidence for the Afterlife.* Guildford, UK: White Crow Books, 2013.

Index